KT-468-042

JIVING AT THE CROSSROADS

with a new Afterword

John Waters

TRANSWORLD IRELAND

TRANSWORLD IRELAND
an imprint of The Random House Group Limited
20 Vauxhall Bridge Road, London SW1V 2SA
www.transworldbooks.co.uk

First published in 1991 by The Blackstaff Press Ltd
Published with a new Afterword in 2011 by Transworld Ireland,
a division of Transworld Publishers

A CIP catalogue record for this book
is available from the British Library.

ISBN 9781848271272

Addresses for Random House Group Ltd companies outside the UK
can be found at: www.randomhouse.co.uk
The Random House Group Ltd Reg. No. 954009

The Random House Group Limited supports the Forest Stewardship
Council® (FSC®), the leading international forest-certification organization.
All our titles printed on Greenpeace-approved FSC®-certified paper carry
the FSC® logo. Our paper procurement policy can be found
at www.randomhouse.co.uk/environment

Typeset in 11/14pt Sabon by
Kestrel Data, Exeter, Devon.
Printed and bound by
CPI Group (UK) Ltd, Croydon, CR0 4YY.

2 4 6 8 10 9 7 5 3 1

LL

Diarmaid Ferriter

'A seminal book'
Eamon Dunphy

'John Waters' method is the word, his passion truth, his object a
better world . . . a wonderful, witty, and moving book'
Patsy McGarry, *Irish Press*

'Riveting and engrossing' – Seán Dunne, *Cork Examiner*

'He has written a terrific book. I beg you to buy it'
James Downey, *Irish Independent*

'An honest, funny, courageous book . . . the writer has indeed
a heart with considerable idealism and passion . . . both calm
and outrageous, funny and serious, mild and brave. *Jiving at the
Crossroads* is one of the liveliest and most incisive books I've read
this year. The book is shot through with a sense of excited and
exciting discovery of many things and people . . . John Waters is
one of the most credible and refreshing of all Irish journalists'
Brendan Kennelly, *Irish Times*

'This [is a] rich, racily written first book . . . one of
the most inspired/inspiring debuts to have come
from an Irish journalist in recent years'
Aubrey Malone, *Sunday Independent*

'Bristles with indignation'
Gerald Dawe, *Fortnight*

'This is a splendid book, warm, eloquent and calmly intelligent, as
easy and rewarding a read as anything published recently in Ireland.
It combines political analysis, polemical essay, personal reminiscence
and recapitulation of pieces published in the past . . . marvellously
evocative of an era drawing to a close . . . This is the best book
about Fianna Fáil published in recent years, and by a mile the
best-written. A lot of it is funny, but mostly it's very sad'
Eamonn McCann, *Sunday Tribune*

'One of the most original and insightful Irish non-fiction
books of the last decade . . . Any commentator who claims to
know how Irish people feel, particularly about the national
question, should be made to read this book'
Conor Foley, *Tribune Magazine*

www.transworldbooks.co.uk
www.transworldireland.ie

John Waters has been a respected columnist with the *Irish Times* for over twenty years. As well as *Jiving at the Crossroads* (Blackstaff, 1991) his books include *Race of Angels: Ireland and the Genesis of U2* (Blackstaff/Fourth Estate, 1994); *Every Day Like Sunday?* (Poolbeg, 1995); *An Intelligent Person's Guide to Modern Ireland* (Duckworth, 1997); *The Politburo Has Decided That You Are Unwell* (Liffey Press, 2004); *Lapsed Agnostic* (Continuum, 2007); *Beyond Consolation* (Continuum, 2010); and *Feckers: 50 People Who Fecked Up Ireland* (Constable, 2010).

To my mother and sisters
and the memory of my father

'History is not a tale told by the fireside. It is an ever-developing process, and all its events not so much events as thoughts hammered into mortal heads.'

from *The Irish*, Sean O'Faolain

Contents

INTRODUCTION

At the End of the Age of Innocence

In the middle of a large lunchtime crowd in a shopping
mall in Cork, on 26 October 1990, I found myself being
carried inexorably in the direction of Brian Lenihan. With
my notebook in one hand and a biro in the other, I was
attempting to cover the Fianna Fáil candidate's canvass in
a detached, dispassionate manner. But something in the air
seemed to make this impossible. Most of the time, in the
whirlpool of the crowd, it was difficult merely to remain
upright. From time to time, the hands of the presidential
candidate, bruised and reddened from human contact,
were raised in acknowledgement of that which, though
sensed by all, was intangible, ineffable. The crowd, mostly
women, besieged the candidate, reaching out to touch
him, kiss him, slap his back, whisper words of solace,
encouragement, love. It should have been hard to get close
to him, but instead it seemed impossible to avoid being
swept towards some kind of contact. It had been the same
everywhere he had been since getting off the plane in Cork
that morning. As the campaign bus drove through the city,
people waved and smiled, clapped their hands and honked

their hooters. An old woman, standing on the pavement in Patrick Street, had raised a clenched fist and shouted, on the verge of tears, 'God bless you, Brian.'

Since leaving Dublin, I had been keeping out of the candidate's way. There was too much to be said, too many complexities, too much history, too much emotion, and few or no words with which to say anything. We had confined ourselves to the occasional exchange of winks. But now, in the heat of the crowd, we found ourselves almost cheek-to-cheek. 'The Irish are an extraordinary people,' he said. 'How do you mean?' I asked. 'They love me. Did you ever see anything like it?' 'No,' I replied, truthfully. It occurred to me that he seemed surprised that people did seem still to love him. In an instant I found that I had put a protective arm around his shoulders. 'It's great,' I said. 'Why wouldn't they?' With that, the candidate was swept away again in the milling throng.

Later, a colleague on the campaign trail made the same observation and was equally incredulous. 'My God!' she exclaimed. 'They love him. I can't believe it!' I asked her if she could look at Brian Lenihan and seriously find herself in agreement with the pronouncements she had been reading in the newspapers over the past couple of days – that he was corrupt, crooked, an ogre of some kind? She made no comment, presumably not wishing to question the illusion that she and others had created for themselves: they liked the equation just the way it was.

For the previous week, much of which I had spent in the candidate's company, the response to the party's canvass had been lukewarm at best. If public enthusiasm was a necessary ingredient of success, Brian Lenihan was going to lose the election by a mile. The turnout around the country had been largely of party faithful: old soldiers with peaked caps and weather-beaten faces. They listened politely as the candidate regaled them with talk of the necessity for an 'inspirational presidency', which would give 'non-executive leadership' and 'represent the national ethos'.

The pattern had been similar everywhere we went. In contrast to the Mary Robinson gatherings, one rarely saw a face much under forty, except for the children who came along to get the headbands with the legend, 'Home and Away the Best Team'.

Judging from his occasional faraway expression, Lenihan had noticed that something was amiss, but there was always someone nearby with a ready rationalisation: they were catching people at the wrong time of day, the weather was not great, and anyway the opinion polls were holding up. To some extent the fault was with the Fianna Fáil organisation, which seemed to be taking the outcome as a foregone conclusion. Apathy and complacency ruled the day. If nobody said anything, one could not help thinking, they would have lost the election before they knew what had hit them.

But now something odd had shifted in the psyche of the Irish public, one of those quirks of psychology that make Irish politics turn grey the heads of those who earn their livings writing about them. The cycle had begun four days before, when Brian Lenihan had been manoeuvred into saying, on live television, that he had not phoned President Hillery in January 1982 to try to put pressure on him to refuse a dissolution of the Dáil to the outgoing Taoiseach, Garret FitzGerald. Within those few days, a tape had been produced of an interview Lenihan had given, six months earlier, to a postgraduate student, in which he had said that he had made such a phone call. Then, in a frenzy of hurt and confusion, the candidate had gone back on television, his political armour uncharacteristically askew, to state that his previous television appearance had conveyed the correct impression: he had not phoned the president. That was his 'mature recollection' of the events in question.

In the eyes of the media and Dublin-based opinion-formers, Brian Lenihan became public enemy number one. What Lenihan's political godson, Sean Doherty, had once described as 'the wild, unbridled madnesses' were on the loose. Leader writers and columnists held forth at great length on the necessity for truth in public life. They declared Lenihan an unfit person to be president of Ireland. They called for high standards in high places, though they did not feel the need to extend this call to embrace the Fine Gael people who had successfully laid the trap into which Lenihan had fallen.

A whole part of Ireland, of Irish life, seemed to speak again with a single voice. It was the voice of an impatient people – a voice with a discreet but determined purpose – and Lenihan was now in the path of its pointed venom. It was the voice of a people whose views had been forged in the white heat of their hatred for Fianna Fáil, a people who had pulled themselves away from their roots, who had scraped the last trace of cowdung from their souls. They were well-educated and had been to university and studied concepts like dialectical materialism, positivism, gradualism, and democratic centralism. They had long been appalled at the fact that their own country refused to reveal itself in terms of the learning they had accumulated. They wanted to squeeze the nation's politics into the neat packets of their own understanding. The Lenihan 'lie' had been manna from heaven. Here was a cut-and-dried case: a Fianna Fáil politician caught red-handed telling untruths. All the sins of Fianna Fáil politicians past and present became telescoped into this single 'lie'; it had become a symbol for everything that these people wished to eradicate from the Irish body politic.

One of the great bugbears of such people was what they described as 'the artificial division of the civil war'. To listen to them in a casual manner was to imagine that they were opposed, body and soul, to division of any kind. But after a time it might occur to you that what they really meant was that they did not like the old division because it was uncongenial. Just as they did not appear to have as clear a definition of 'truth' as they did of 'lies', they wished the concept of division to be putty in their hands. They did not like the idea of the division based on the civil war, but appeared determined to create a newer, more resilient division to replace it. This was the division between themselves – the people who wanted Ireland to be different than it was, who wanted it to conform immediately to some paradigm in their heads – and the people who were happy to let it evolve at its own pace and in its own way. When the rest of the country resisted their attempts to manhandle it into their new, idealised Ireland, they went away to sulk in the snugs of southside Dublin, and emerged on the radio to talk among themselves about what they had decided to do.

It did not seem to occur to them that the people of Ireland might be more open to change and progress if from time to time they were asked for an opinion or were made to feel entitled to participate in the creation of this promised land.

The tragedy of modern Ireland was that progress had been allowed to become synonymous with one class, a class that appeared to specialise in making itself obnoxious to the rest of the country. To more and more people, rightly or wrongly, this class was becoming known as 'Dublin 4'. All that was required was that, for once, the two sides might find themselves wanting the same thing, even if for different reasons, and that the mutual nature of this desire might be concealed from either side until its object had been attained.

The presidential election had come to present such an opportunity. I was sure that Mary Robinson knew she could win, in spite of the pundits. I also knew, from my trips home to County Roscommon, that the most surprising people were talking of voting for her. All they needed was to taste her confidence, to sense her will to win. Dublin 4, however, had got used to losing, and was perhaps even a little in love with it. It derived so much pleasure out of being able to berate the rest of the country for its backwardness that it had excluded the possibility of the entire country ever being able to move forward together. It was prepared to go on losing, so long as this allowed it to feel superior. It had adopted Mary Robinson largely because it thought her another martyr to the great 'liberal', 'pluralist', and/or 'progressive' cause.

There were times when almost everyone seemed to have a different notion of what the Robinson candidacy meant. If, in the autumn of 1990, you had traversed the spiritual territory of Dublin 4, trying to gauge the nature of Mary Robinson's support, you would have become very confused indeed. Even within the Labour Party, which had nominated Robinson for the presidency, there were two distinct points of view as to the meaning of her candidacy. Party leader Dick Spring and the people around him were at pains to express their desire to move into the centre of the Irish political field. Over on the Labour left, however, there existed an altogether different analysis. The reason they eventually threw their support behind the Robinson campaign, they were anxious to stress, was because she was the Trojan Horse of the left. Her unique appeal for the liberal middle classes would allow the left to crack, for the first time, the stranglehold of the conservative parties on that constituency. Everyone was looking forward to a different definition of success. It occurred to me that a candidacy instilled with such a sense of vagueness was perfectly placed to appeal to the fevered babble of modern Ireland.

I had started out wanting Mary Robinson to win. She was clever and impressive: her candidacy seemed like a good idea. I believed that she had a good chance of winning. Anything was now possible in Irish politics, because people had begun to look around them, to connect the everyday happenings in their lives with the nature of their political culture, and were coming to decisions in a measured and intelligent way. I could see a fair proportion of the people of Roscommon, the people who had voted out Sean Doherty in the 1989 general election, voting to put Mary Robinson in.

I had one infallible touchstone. I thought about what my father might have thought of Mary Robinson. He would have admired her intelligence, her achievement, her poise. 'She's a real lady,' he would have said. I thought of other people I knew, and was astounded to find that I could visualise them voting for her as well.

All that could prevent this happening, I was convinced, was if something happened to galvanise such people against her, to resurrect the old divisions and stake out the 'two Irelands' of which the people on the radio loved to speak.

Few of the people on the radio, or indeed the writers in the newspapers, gave Mary Robinson much chance. From the outset, the consensus had been that she might come a respectable third, with perhaps a few percentage points more than the normal Labour Party vote. Her supporters' lack of faith, from her point of view, was a huge asset. Only when you became a serious contender were you obliged to carry the banner of Dublin 4. As an outsider, she was free to make and pursue her own agenda. The longer she had to make herself known to the voters, one by one, without having to ask them to take sides, the better chance she had of getting them on hers. By starting her campaign a good four months before the others, and in the highly symbolic location of the village of Allihies in west Cork, she had already shown herself to have an acute grasp of the necessity for both covering miles and underlining meanings.

I had my reservations about Mary Robinson, but when I thought about them, I recognised them as petty, small-town reservations. I saw her at first as someone who, if she had been from my home town of Castlerea, would have lived at the better end of town, would have gone away to boarding school, and would not have mixed with the girls and boys from Main Street. She was the kind of person whom, sometime in the dim and distant past, we had all aspired to be. Behind her intimidating intellect, she seemed shy. We could do with a president who was shy.

But could she win? No, said the conventional wisdom. As the 'left-wing' candidate, she was, the pundits assured us, a no-hoper. The only issue to be decided was whether her transfers would be enough to give the Fine Gael candidate a chance of catching Lenihan on the second count.

Ironically, Fine Gael began to suspect that Mary Robinson might win long before many of her own supporters. Or, rather, they suspected that they would lose, that the mantle of first runner-up might pass from their grasp for the first time. The Robinson campaign was complex and mysterious: it seemed to contain too many of the dialectics and contradictions of modern Ireland. It was too up-to-date. It had left them behind.

Fine Gael was more comfortable with the way things had been: when there were just Good Guys and Bad Guys, and they shared the spoils between them. Being beaten by Fianna Fáil was uncomfortable and disappointing when it happened, but it was never shameful and there would always be another day. Yet here, on the horizon, was a total outsider beginning to look just a little too sure of what she was about. Fine Gael needed to get the game back to the way it had been before, to the clear-cut divisions between Good Guys and Bad Guys, between truth and lies, between Charlie, The Great National Bastard, and Garret the Good.

Around the beginning of September 1990, just as the possibility of her winning became the merest whiff on the wind, I went to interview Mary Robinson in her home in Ranelagh, on the south side of Dublin. We talked about her career in politics, her vision of the presidency, all nondescript stuff that she would deal with in a thousand interviews during the campaign. My interview would never be published, and for the most part this was not a significant loss to the public record. There was little in the way of exciting copy, certainly nothing like the content of the interview she would later give to my old magazine, *Hot Press*, in which, while declaring herself a practising Catholic, she attacked the 'patriarchal, male-dominated presence of the Catholic Church'. Our most animated exchanges were on the subject of our mutual admiration for the president of Czechoslovakia, Vaclav Havel.

Yet Mary Robinson said one thing that stuck in my brain. If she could succeed in communicating it to the people of Ireland, I knew that it would win her the presidency. It made sense of all the seemingly contradictory things she had said elsewhere, about Catholicism, about socialism, about progressive politics, about the view the Irish people needed to have of themselves. 'I'm a Catholic from Mayo,' she said. 'There's nothing about *that* Ireland that I don't know. So it's me. I understand it from within and I want to develop it on, but in the way that one would want to develop oneself, almost. I don't repudiate so much as want to coax along into a different mould.' In this statement, I was convinced, lay the key not just to Mary Robinson's chances of being elected president, but to the future of Irish politics.

Here was a woman who belonged to the liberal tradition of Irish politics, who came from a bourgeois family in the West of Ireland, but who as a lawyer had pursued the interests of the poor and underprivileged. Though remaining a Catholic, she had been led by her political activities into conflict with the Church's position on several issues. As often as not, she had been on the losing side. And yet, in this declaration, she was saying that there did not have to be winners or losers, there did not have to be sides. By fighting against the perceived conservative forces in Irish society, she had come to appreciate the nature of those forces: that they were not merely the preserve of a diehard minority, but an essential part of the equilibrium of the society. Conversely, the liberal forces to which Dublin 4 had claimed ownership did not belong to them alone. Conservatism and liberalism were not exterior forces, but intrinsic parts of herself, of her own experience and outlook; just as they were parts of me, of all of us.

There was scope, she believed, even within what she described as the 'modest parameters' of the presidency, to be a catalyst for change in the country, without seeming to attack people for their cultures and their sincerely held beliefs. 'There are no overall certitudes in Ireland anymore,' she said. 'There's a lot of diversity of thinking, a lot of uncertainty, a lot of trying to assimilate to other cultures. It's a time when we need to take stock, to look into our hearts and find a sense of Irishness, to find a pride in ourselves that will make us sure of where we are.'

I tiptoed out of the room, afraid of disturbing her perfect train of thought. This was the way to get where we all wanted to go. She was not a leader in the conventional sense, but she had located a part of herself that we all had in common: the need to live together in one small country and feel that we are members of a single multifarious people.

But then Fine Gael stuck the boot in. They weren't going to win, so they decided to burst the ball. The wild, unbridled madnesses took hold. From Mary Robinson's viewpoint, the Lenihan phone-call controversy had to be the worst thing that could have happened. She had been quietly going about the country, gathering up her votes in ones and twos, when suddenly we were back in 1982, the year of the GUBU. Fine Gael had won that encounter, and any rematch on that particular pitch, they reckoned, just had to be good news for them. In any event, they had very little to lose. The muck flew thick and dirty. The media joined in the fun, some more than others. Among those who threw the largest clods were journalists who had aligned themselves with the Robinson campaign. This could have been fatal: to her.

But Robinson herself seemed to be inspired. Throughout her campaign she had been stressing the role of the president as being 'outside politics'. To the ears of a country sickened by the chicanery of politicians on one hand, and the sanctimonious finger-wagging of Dublin 4 on the other, it was a felicitous phrase. Politics had somehow grown away from the people: they themselves felt 'outside politics'.

The instinct of a politician would have been to join in the mêlée. For Mary Robinson to do so would have suited Fine Gael: they liked mêlées and occasionally came out of them on top. But she seemed to be aware that this was not her row. She remained silent, though silence might not have been enough. The issue was already in danger of turning into another battle of Us and Them, of the 'old' versus the 'new' Irelands.

Dublin 4 had never forgiven Charlie Haughey for having been the one to bail them out of the mess created by years of madness in Irish politics. Dublin 4 had always hated Haughey and had begun to hate itself for needing him. It longed to be able to let off a little of the steam of its self-loathing. Haughey it could not touch, but Lenihan, his closest political ally, was fair game. All the better that the 'issue', the Great Untruth, originated in the GUBU era, the period for which Dublin 4 had reluctantly had to give the Fianna Fáil leader absolution. What could be more symbolic? They would call for another sacrifice, and would then be able to live with themselves – and with Haughey – for a while longer.

The Progressive Democrats would be the Salome to demand the sacrifice. It was done: Lenihan was sacked from the cabinet. The issue of the Great Untruth was still unresolved. Brian Lenihan was still the Fianna Fáil candidate, but, miraculously, the finger-wagging hordes pronounced themselves satisfied with the blood-letting.

We began to do what the organisers of the plot against Lenihan had wanted: we began to take sides. On the Sunday following the unleashing of the tapes controversy, I met Mary Robinson in Killarney, to interview her over breakfast for the *Irish Times*. This is a part of what I wrote the next day:

There is a sense in which having breakfast with Mary Robinson is the same as having breakfast on your own. There is a sense in which having breakfast with any of the three candidates would be like having breakfast on your own. For this election does not so much offer three alternative individuals as three separate but distinct parts of each one of us, vying for the upper hand.

This election is about which aspect of ourselves we really want to come out on top. Brian Lenihan is the way we have always been; Austin Currie represents what we profess to aspire to, but don't really; and Mary

Robinson is that part of us which wishes to make a firm purpose of amendment.

There is a part of all of us, if we're honest, that knows that Brian Lenihan's 'sin' is no more than a recurrence of the original sin of Irish politics, a part that feels obliged to support a man of Austin Currie's courage and background, and a part that wants desperately to cling to the opportunity offered by Mary Robinson for a complete break with the past.

For a while there it appeared that the latter part would win out on the day. So much so that I had been looking forward to telling my grandchildren that I'd had breakfast with Mary Robinson in Killarney, even as the wall was tumbling down, a wall which existed as much within myself as on the Irish political landscape. But as I climbed the stairs of the Great Southern Hotel, it was impossible not to be aware of the feverish rebuilding operation being mounted by the traditional forces within the mysterious psyche of Irish politics.

The morning papers were full of the accounts of the efforts of the great master builders – Garret FitzGerald, Desmond O'Malley, Bertie Ahern – to rebuild the wall which they would lead us to believe stood between truth and lies, standards high and low, integrity and shame, Us and Them. If I were Mary Robinson, I reflected, I would be anxious to keep my hands clean, to go on pointing out that the wall had been built in the wrong place to begin with, and very probably without planning permission.

I said something along the lines of the above to Mary Robinson. She replied that she had read my article about the reception Lenihan had received in Cork, and handed me a statement she had just released to the press. It began: 'The phone-call controversy should not be blown out of proportion or detract from the decency of Brian Lenihan's record of public service or be allowed to plunge the country into a government crisis.' The statement seemed to me to be perfectly pitched: victory for Mary Robinson would be achieved not by opposing or condemning the forces she must defeat, but by respecting and accommodating them, by adapting the strengths and correcting the follies of the past.

For the final ten days of the presidential campaign, it seemed as though the tapes affair was occurring to provide a metaphor for what we had become as a people. Sometimes you felt you were observing events and voices inside your own head, that the candidates and their actions were all part of a dream that was bound up inextricably with your own history. And, just as sometimes you get the feeling that you can change the course of a dream by waking up, you felt that you could alter the course of the election, and of history, by a word, a gesture, a stroke on a piece of paper. As the action of the campaign went this way and that, the forces that conspired to dictate its shape were not the block prejudices of whole sections of society, but the ordinary, everyday feelings of individuals. Never had Irish politics felt so close to the individual human being, so subject to whim, so open to aspiration, prejudice, emotion. Never before had an individual vote seemed so capable of expressing such complexities, so connected to oneself and one's past, one's history. It was a metaphor, yes, but it was also real. It was a metaphor for a reality that was under our noses. It was history registering on our lives the changes it had made while we were not paying attention.

I believed that what was happening made a certain sense of its own, but that this sense was in grave danger of being distorted by the interpretations that would be put on it by those who wished to deny the past almost in its entirety. It was odd, listening daily to all this talk about 'values', 'morality' and 'high standards', to be able to detect no evidence of these admirable qualities in the actions of those who articulated them. It seemed to me that we were at a turning point in our history, but that there was a distinct possibility that we were being diverted down an avenue of expediency no better than that from which we were now voluntarily emerging. By pointing the finger at Brian Lenihan, the Dublin 4 pharisees were pointing also at all those who in the past had voted or otherwise supported him politically, who had felt a twinge of sympathy in his recent illness, who had even allowed their faces to crease into a smile at some incidence of his celebrated buffoonery. Moreover, by doing so, they were driving back into the tribal ghettoes those who had been on the point of emerging. Thus, they were not merely acting in a manner that was unjust and dishonest, they were indulging in behaviour that was counter-productive to their own expressed interests.

I had definite reasons for believing this to be so. For most of my adult life I had lived in a political culture that was defined by politicians like Brian Lenihan. For much of that time, I too had been impatient with that culture. From the moment I reached voting age, my political existence, in so far as I had one, was centred on the figure of Sean Doherty, our local TD in Roscommon. Doherty, as they say in all the best newspaper profiles, was 'no stranger to controversy', but at election time he invariably came in at the top of the poll. For years this had both baffled and infuriated me. I, too, had begun to look upon my fellow citizens as backward and irrational. Then, after spending a few years in Dublin, I went back one day and found myself scrambling to catch them up.

Although a little more than a decade older than myself, Sean Doherty was a politician in the old style. He had learned that style at the lap of the master. Through the political activities of his father, a Fianna Fáil county councillor, Doherty had spent much of his boyhood in the company of politicians, of none more so than Lenihan, the local TD from 1961 to 1973 and sometime government minister. Ever since Doherty's own entry into politics, Lenihan had been his political godfather within Fianna Fáil, advising him, promoting him, and licking his wounds when things went wrong.

During the 1990 presidential election, covering Brian Lenihan's campaign for the *Irish Times*, I had occasion to listen carefully to the way he spoke, to the things he said. I soon realised that he was the old block off which Sean Doherty was a chip.

I had often noticed the way people who were opposed to the idea of politicians like Brian Lenihan would accuse him of talking in gobbledegook. They objected to the fact that he did not appear to answer questions directly, that he prevaricated, that he even told lies. This would become the central issue of the presidential election. But it always seemed to me that he was one of the most careful speakers that I had ever come across, even better than Doherty, who had learned the basics from him but had never learned to convey his meaning without other signals such as nods and winks.

Brian Lenihan winked, but not in the same way as Doherty. It was not a conspiratorial wink; it was used, albeit subconsciously, to denote the arrival of the participants at a common understanding. Doherty's wink invited you to join in the shafting of his enemies; Lenihan's merely recognised the existence of a common, unstated purpose. Doherty's wink was a necessary accompaniment to verbal communication; Lenihan only winked when there was no need to speak.

Lenihan, I always believed, was a lot smarter than he was generally given credit for. Whenever he spoke, he had a way of conveying everything he wanted to convey without seeming to utter a word of it. It was like algebra: you calculated everything that someone in Lenihan's position might be expected to say, you subtracted everything he had said, and what you were left with was what he had meant to convey. Journalists were annoyed because he had seemed to answer their questions with a series of further questions, enigmatic phrases and bland declarations. Those to whom he had been speaking, who knew the codes, were left in no doubt as to his position.

Many times during the presidential campaign, I found myself wondering in equations: if Lenihan says that x minus one plus y minus two is equal to y squared, then what does x equal? Lenihan, I noticed, replied to questions with great care and often at great length. The answer he gave did not always appear to be to the question he had been asked, but that did not mean that his reply did not contain the shape of the answer he wished to convey.

He had a way of defusing every potentially problematic

question before answering it. To the uninitiated, talking to Lenihan was a bit like talking on a very bad telephone line. He seemed to pick up on the most innocuous phrase of the question, sometimes just a single word, and build his reply around that. So, if you asked him on the day after he had been sacked from the cabinet by his friend Charles Haughey: 'Mr Lenihan, what is now your opinion of your party leader, Mr Haughey?' he might reply: 'Mr Haughey is the democratically elected leader of the Fianna Fáil party and as such has my full support.' It did not take a genius to work out, from what was missing from this endorsement, that Brian Lenihan was not exactly in love with his leader.

I got into trouble with several Dublin friends and acquaintances for writing in the *Irish Times* during the campaign that Brian Lenihan is actually 'among the most truthful of politicians, because he possesses the irrefutable integrity of innocence'. Some people thought I was joking, since the main issue of the campaign had been the lies that Brian Lenihan allegedly had told about phoning, or not phoning, President Hillery. I could not get people to understand that even when Lenihan appears to be stalling and bluffing, he is sending out clear signals as to his true feelings. If you knew the codes, you could read him like a book. Even when what he was saying sounded meaningless, his true opinion could be deduced from analysing his repetition of the same phrases, with exactly the same emphasis, again and again. He was the worst liar I had ever seen, certainly a lot worse than many of the journalists who were now excoriating him.

I was not joking either when I wrote that 'when other politicians accuse Brian Lenihan of telling lies, it is they who are being dishonest'. Lenihan's use of language was just one of the tools essential to the trade of politician in the age to which he belonged. These tools were as vital as the handshake, which caused Brian Lenihan's right hand to become raw and blistered in the course of the presidential campaign, and the sense of irony which cushioned him from the far greater pain that might have come from the attacks on his integrity. Sean Doherty in the past had delighted in telling a favourite story about the Brian Lenihan who had trained him in the trade of politics. 'Brian,' Doherty asked him once, 'did you ever tell a lie in the House?' 'My dear boy,' replied Lenihan, 'the only place to tell a lie is in the House!' One of the results of the 1990 presidential election campaign was that no politician would feel safe any longer in assuming that such a remark would be taken in the ironic spirit in which it had been made.

Even journalists whose stock-in-trade was a similar irony had suddenly become very solemn, as though they had been rumbled walking between the lines on the pavement. 'What Brian Lenihan did', wrote one such journalist – Colm Tóibín in the *Sunday Independent* – 'should not be judged in isolation; it is part of a system, and a system that we can all do without in the future.' This system, Colm Tóibín said, was 'when misleading the public became a way of life for members of his party'. For such people, Lenihan had now to bear not just the sins of his own past but those of his party, his leaders past and present, and all the wrongs, real or imagined, that Fianna Fáil had inflicted on the people of Ireland. No more could Lenihan be the jolly giant of Irish politics. Those who had lain in wait for Fianna Fáil for half their lifetimes were now playing it by the book, were calling in all the old markers.

There was a price for this new literalism. From the very moment when the issue of the phone call to Áras an Uachtaráin had first surfaced on an RTE television programme, Brian Lenihan had had to suspend the sense of irony that had protected him for a lifetime in politics. I asked him, one day towards the end of the campaign, why he no longer made jokes. I had seen him on television and had noticed that he did not try to deflate his opponents with the pinpricks of humour that had long been his speciality, or even to make jokes at his own expense. He replied that he was now afraid to crack jokes because his sense of humour was likely to be wilfully misconstrued.

There was no place, it seemed, for irony in the new, squeaky-clean world of Dublin 4. Everything was rational, humourless, black-and-white, to be taken literally, except when they decided otherwise.

I switched on the radio one lunchtime at the height of the debate about the lie that Lenihan supposedly had told. Garret FitzGerald was talking about integrity in politics, a theme that, somehow, he had made his own political refrain. He was talking about the public perception that all politicians told lies. This was untrue, he said. Politicians did not tell lies as a rule: what sometimes occurred was that a politician might not tell the full truth, or might enter a caveat into what he had said. This, Garret FitzGerald appeared to believe, was different from telling a lie, and was therefore quite acceptable.

Irish politics had become a battlefield, and the truth a ploughshare beaten into a double-edged sword. A couple of nights before polling day, a group of Irish writers and intellectuals appeared on the BBC 2 arts and media programme *The Late Show* to talk about the meaning of what was happening. They spoke of Fianna Fáil as though it were some dark spirit that once had hung around the Irish landscape, but was now, mercifully, on the run. Colm Tóibín (for it was he) celebrated the advent of a new 'rationalism', represented by Mary Robinson.

In those days in the late autumn of 1990, the concept of truth seemed to lose all meaning. Brian Lenihan and his supposed lie, whenever and to whomever that lie had been told, became the weapon with which the two peoples of modern Ireland seemed set to beat each other to death. The 'lie' did not matter: it was a symbol of something much larger. Nobody could quite say what the lie had been, or at what precise moment it had been told, or what it was about, or how important it was, but everyone had an opinion about what should happen to the man who supposedly had told it. And yet this man, just a few short months before, had been by general agreement the most popular politician in the country. What could it all mean?

I began to wonder; should this tawdry episode be written into history, how, in a couple of generations, might we explain it to our grandchildren? What could we expect them to absorb about it? What was it really about? Would we be able to keep a straight face while we explained to them that a naughty politician had tried to ring the president one night in 1982, and that, almost a decade later, the questions of whether he had or had not came to be seen as a very serious thing? Would we be able to tell them for sure whether Brian Lenihan had rung Áras an Uachtaráin, and if we were not, would this represent any deficiency in their grasp of the history of 1990s Ireland?

And what would we tell them was the 'moral' of the story? That politicians who tell lies were not allowed to prosper in the Ireland we had created? I figured that if we were to tell them that this is what the events of the 1990 presidential election campaign were about, they would laugh all the way to the bathroom to be sick.

That is why I have written this book. It is not an argument; it is a story. That it is true is neither here nor there; it is the story I will read to my putative grandchildren when they ask me what I remember about my own youth. It is my attempt to record what Ireland was really like before we finally caved in to the wishes of those loud-voiced ones among us with no stomach for the past.

For many years now we have listened to politicians and political commentators lamenting the negative aspects of Irish politics: the primacy of the 'parish pump', clientelism, 'stroke' politics, buck-leppery, and so on. They speak as though Irish politics is some form of disease afflicting the majority of the population. And not only do the alternatives they advocate not seem any better, or more moral, than that which they decry, but the very rudeness of their interventions actually appears to put a brake on the changes that are taking place organically in Irish politics.

Mary Robinson proved that, in moving towards a 'new Ireland', it is neither necessary nor advisable to leave the 'old Ireland' behind. The past is the reason we are here – politically as much as otherwise. It is the stuff of our political culture, just as we ourselves are the flesh and blood of our ancestors. How can we know where we want to go if we refuse to acknowledge the place whence we came? The past is made up, not of dates and names and battles and conquests as in the history books, but of images, colours, tastes and longings from our everyday lives. We cannot know what we believe, or why, by referring to an index of dates, or listening to the pundits of history on a radio show. That, as perhaps never before, is likely to grate with our own sense of reality and truth.

This book is an attempt to tell what I believe about Irish politics, and to show, in my own way, the lessons borne out by the Robinson victory: that politics is about real people and that change comes about, not through the intervention of political experts or deities, but in the hearts and minds of people who, in the arrogance of my own profession, are described as ordinary. Only if we surrender our sense of politics as something human and everyday will politics cease to serve our needs as human beings.

1

Procession

The torchlight procession moved slowly down Main Street, the flames from the burning sticks dancing in the March night air.

A chilled whisper ran down the town's spine.

'He's coming!'

'*Tá sé ag teacht!*' The excitement of this exclamation, borrowed from a television advert for Guinness, was buried under layers of irony and mockery.

'He's coming!' This voice respectful and insistent.

'Who's coming?'

'Doherty. He's coming!'

'Fuck Doherty!'

'*Tá sé ag teacht!*'

I sat in the Hiace van with Dermo, waiting by the side of the street, as though for an approaching funeral. We counted ourselves among the hostile ones.

There was no music, no razzmatazz, just a low hum of conversation, a shuffle of footwear, growing louder all the time. The word 'procession' was apposite: the approaching swarm of people was such as occurred in the town only on

35

religious occasions – either funerals or the annual Corpus Christi procession from the Church to the fair green, opposite where we sat. We watched, too, as we would watch a passing funeral – staring straight ahead but with eyes on swivels to pick up every nuance.

The Hiace was a warm cocoon of heat and sound. The engine remained running, but beneath the throb of the stereocassette its smooth growl was next to inaudible. Dermo had put on one of his favourite albums, Bruce Springsteen's *Darkness on the Edge of Town*, and its energised melancholy penetrated our two bodies like an x-ray.

> Through the mansions of fear, through the mansions
>   of pain,
> See my daddy walking through them factory gates
>   in the rain.
> Factory takes his youth, factory gives him life,
> The workin', the workin', just the workin' life.

The music shut out the world of the street. Something in the poetry of the language allowed it to transcend the mundaneness of the worlds it both conjured up for you and inoculated you against. It spoke to you in two languages at once – the broad strokes of the macro-cultural language of mainstream rock and roll, which allowed it to seep into the lives of people at opposite ends of the globe, and the everyday nuances of your own life, which it seemed to have no right to understand. It was the language through which people like Dermo and I communicated with one another; it allowed us to sidestep the ordinary and the everyday. It plugged directly into the rhythm we had created for our own lives. It wrapped sameness in a cloak of evocation and mystery, and supplanted vain ambition with seductive aspiration. It reinvented life as a dream with an inescapably happy ending.

Every spare moment of our lives was spent either listening to records, reading about the bands and artists who made them, or talking about what the music signified. For us, rock and roll was a living language, and a part of its appeal was its incomprehensibility to those who were not attuned to its rhythms, sounds and tempos, its tragic narcissism, its exuberant drama. Such people had their own language, the language of sport, perhaps, which Dermo understood but I did not, or politics, which I had a smattering of but which for him was a dead language.

But now, in the second week of March 1982, the insistent babble of that language bore defiantly down upon us. The procession drew near, its speed between a walk and a trot. The party was late by almost an hour and had many more stops before the night was out. The faithful of such places as Ballintubber and Roscommon had yet to have their moments to savour the concept of Minister Doherty, to admire the sleek black Mercedes that brought up the rear. The faces flickered their way by, and yet were frozen in space, caught in the dancing torchlight. Most were faces we knew, local Fianna Fáil activists, some of whom we had been at school with. There were people of different ages, shapes and sizes, though they were almost exclusively men.

They came from all types of background, and worked at many different things: there were farmers – mostly 'small' – tradesmen, a postman, shop assistants, a couple of shopkeepers, cattle dealers, a vet, several publicans, a few who were unemployed, and the inevitable host of school-children. Tonight was one of those times, few enough in a small town, when they all found common purpose. Their party had just been returned to office after the aberration of a short period of Fine Gael/Labour coalition government, which had collapsed on an attempt to tax children's shoes. Their champion, Sean Doherty, had been appointed Minister for Justice, a full minister after only five years in the Dáil. They were united as priests concelebrating a Mass of the Resurrection. They were the dogs whose day had finally arrived.

To the passing throng, Dermo and I were not merely Dermot Carroll, joiner's apprentice, soccer player and music fan, and John Waters, mailcar driver and part-time rock journalist. The pair of us, sitting in the green Hiace van opposite Flynn's public house in Main Street, were Blueshirts, and the sons of Blueshirts, to be smiled at as they passed. We stared impassively ahead. The cassette played on.

> Baby, tie your hair back in a long white bow,
> Meet me in the field behind the dynamo,
> You'll hear their voices tellin' you not to go,
> They've made their choices and they'll never know
> What it means to steal, to cheat, to lie,
> What it's like to live and die.

Outside, the music could have been little more than a low, muffled rumble, capable of penetrating nothing, certainly not the consciousnesses of the flush-faced Fianna Fáilers and their triumphant champion, or of spoiling their moment with its pointed accusations. This was their show, and there is no show without Punch. Where was Punch? We wanted to see him too, to be fixed with the triumph in his eyes, to feel the wonder of the moment.

But we did not want him to see us looking. We must stare fixedly ahead, talking out of the sides of our mouths as though nothing was happening. We could have been talking about music, perhaps about an article we had both read in that week's *New Musical Express*. Now the words came automatically from our mouths, without thought, trailing into nonsense, in our attempts to capture the moment without appearing to have any interest.

'That boy Eno is a quare hawk all the same.'

'A terror for the theories, hawh?'

'"Ambient music", no less. He's some boy.' Our eyes swivelled in search of Punch.

As with a funeral, when you scan the faces of the procession behind the hearse and are unable to pick out the one face you are looking for – the wife, husband, brother, sister of the deceased – it was at first impossible to distinguish Doherty in the milling crowd.

You searched and scanned, and as soon as you saw him, you realised that you had been looking at him all along. He had been absorbed into the crowd. There was no spotlight. The dancing flames of the torches picked him out as one of them; he was at once the star and one of the support players. He was the chieftain among his people, and yet was one of them. This perhaps is what we mean when we speak of democracy.

Sean Doherty strode along in the middle of the procession. He was smiling. His face was red and shiny. He was wearing a dark blue suit, with a light pinstripe, a white shirt and dark tie – the regulation uniform of the Fianna

Fáil TD. It alone marked him out from the crowd, most of whom were dressed in sports jackets and trousers and wore no ties.

In the city, I would notice long afterwards, Sean Doherty walked stiffly, with his shoulders slightly hunched, a man away from home. In Dublin, as he walked along, he moved his head sparingly, compensating with eyes that darted hither and thither, missing nothing, constantly looking for clues, like someone with a permanent pain in the neck. But in the country, on his own stomping ground, all the woodenness seemed to fall from him. There was a sprightliness in his step and a flush in his cheeks. He walked easily and without self-consciousness.

They called him 'The Doc', though he was a doctor only in a sense that was vaguely ironic. There was about him a sense of mystery, devilment and danger. He had been a guard and a member of the Special Branch. Stories of his machinations had become legend; he had a reputation for being able to get things done, for looking after 'his own'. Most of these stories were almost certainly apocryphal. It was said that from the time he became Minister of State at the Department of Justice in 1979, all a worried constituent had to do was drop an unwelcome court summons through his letterbox and they would hear no more about it. His supporters would tell you things like this and wink at you, as though they themselves had had occasion to avail of this service; but more often than not it was easy to tell that the individual in question had never been next or near Sean Doherty's letterbox. Their purpose in telling you such things was to make you feel jealous rather than indignant, though if you were indignant as well, they would relish it even more. Now he was Minister for Justice. Their cat had been put in charge of the cupboard with the cream. No wonder they smiled.

Dermo and I had no part in this. We did not belong, or so we thought at the time. We came from 'the other side', and yet we did not belong there either. To us, Doherty represented 'all that was wrong' with Irish politics.

Doherty did not appear to be very clever. He pandered to all the worst instincts in his followers. He had a habit of making what were known as 'smart' remarks, of saying something odd or enigmatic, and winking broadly, sending his followers into paroxysms of laughter. His use of language was strange, as though the compartment that housed his vocabulary had been given a kick and had been twisted around in its seating. Over the previous three election campaigns, I had watched Doherty making his speeches from the backs of lorries in the Market Square in Castlerea. I am unable to remember anything he said, but will never forget the way he said it. Clutching the microphone in his left hand, he would pound the air with his right as he declaimed loudly and with escalating fury, his face growing redder all the while. Words emerged from his mouth as music, a music strange and disturbing.

A journalist wishing to report what Sean Doherty said would on such occasions be at a loss for something to write. Because journalists are wont to assume that the meaning of a speech is vested in the words, they write down the sayings of a politician at such a public gathering and publish them in a newspaper as an account of what occurred, as a summary of the significance of the occasion and the speech.

But the grip of such politicians upon their followers has very little to do with the literal meaning of language.

Doherty rarely if ever spoke from a prepared script, but allowed language to flow out of him as though it had bypassed his reason. He always spoke on a single theme, a theme unspoken and barely defined. It was the theme of solidarity: Us and Them. There was a warmness about him which seemed to come from the redness of his face. It pulled the crowd in like a single-bar electric heater in a railway station waiting room. It embraced believer and curious dissenter alike. It cast a warming and hypnotic spell. The words, in so far as they mattered, conjured up a vaguely defined enemy, an outsider. Sometimes it was 'the Government', sometimes 'the Dublin Establishment', 'the media', 'anti-national interests', or 'the begrudgers'.

Rarely did Doherty make overt attacks on either the sitting Fine Gael member for Roscommon or the entity of Fine Gael as it was understood locally. Always it was 'this government' or 'a certain party'. He had an acute sense of where to place the division, and knew that a goodly number of those listening would have been 'born into' Fine Gael. Occasionally he might mention the 'unseemly' infighting that was going on between the two local Fine Gael candidates, but such mentions, you were given to understand, were made more in sorrow than in anger.

It was something of a mystery to outsiders that the biggest rivalries in the Roscommon constituency were internal to the two main parties. Each of them carefully carved up the territory between their two respective candidates. Castlerea, being along the line of division, was something of a grey area, and consequently was the scene of the occasional brawl between supporters of the two Fine Gael candidates, John Connor and Liam Naughten. It was no secret that Naughten got on much better with

Doherty than with his own running mate, a situation that inevitably contributed to the undercurrents in Doherty's – and indeed Naughten's – public utterances.

Friction within the Fianna Fáil camp tended to manifest itself in a more subtle fashion. Doherty himself has been heard to tell, with undisguised glee, stories about 'putting one over' on his constituency colleague and sometime fellow minister, Terry Leyden.

One Thursday evening, for example, as Doherty was leaving Leinster House to go back down the country, Terry Leyden took him aside and told him that a longtime Fianna Fáil supporter, in his, Leyden's, end of the constituency, had died.

Attendance at funerals is among the first priorities of country TDs mindful of keeping their seats. To be the only deputy to show up for a particular funeral can be a minor coup, and there is much rivalry between politicians in this regard, not all of it playful. For Leyden actually to inform his constituency colleague of this important funeral was in itself a rare instance of generosity. He had seen the death in the paper, he said. The deceased had been a staunch and hard-working party worker and had left a wife and several children. Doherty thanked Leyden for the tip-off. The following evening, Doherty arrived at the corpsehouse to pay his respects. As he was leaving, he shook the bereaved widow's hand and asked, 'Has by any chance Deputy Leyden been along?'

'Oh, yes indeed, Mr Doherty,' the woman replied, 'he was here last night.'

'Oh, good!' exclaimed Doherty. 'Because I told him to come, and he's let me down a couple of times lately.'

When he would tell the story, as he would again and

again, Sean Doherty would wink and laugh delightedly at the sheer gratuitousness of it all.

Now, as he strode through the streets of Castlerea in what would be one of his finest hours, he was laughing again, his face red in the shimmering torchlight.

As the parade passed the two Blueshirts in the Hiace, Dermo reached over and turned the tape up full blast.

> . . . for wanting things that can only be found
> In the darkness on the edge of town,
> In the darkness on the eh . . . eh . . . eh . . . eh . . .
>   edge of town.

Sean Doherty caught my eye and winked in our direction. Dermo turned his head away in disgust. 'Would you look at the head on that? And the price of turnips.'

2

The Man from F.I.N.E. G.A.E.L.

The nature of our political 'beliefs' was always difficult to explain to outsiders. Your 'politics' were a bit like the colour of your eyes: you picked them up from one or both parents, you did not question or even think about them very much, and yet they became part of what other people perceived you to be. They became part of your description.

Small towns in rural Ireland do not have a class structure in the sense that this is understood in the language of modern politics. What they have, as John Healy used to point out, is a hierarchy, in which every family, and every individual, has a fixed place. Everybody knows practically everybody else, and the collective memory in most cases will stretch back over several generations.

The process is complex to the outsider, but second nature to the individual member of the community in question. When two of the town's inhabitants meet in the street, a process occurs in which both are able to flash up in some part of their brains a 'description', a social image, of the other. This unwritten description will include such data as the person's address, occupation, the make of their car, if any, the address and occupations of their parents, the extent of their social activities, their mode of dress, speech and general physical demeanour, and of course, the person's political 'persuasion'. This information will enable both of them to define the nature of their relationship.

In this procedure there is no room for illusion. In an instant, each will have absorbed the available data on the other person and will have placed himself above, below or on a par in the social hierarchy of the town. The process has nothing to do with outward acknowledgements or appearances, in which there is some room for defiance and assertion. This takes place within the very soul of the individual, and holds no place for snobbery or self-deception. Both the individuals in question, in that instant, will have come to the same conclusion as to their relationship. Other than by leaving, it is almost impossible, within the ordinary activity of one's life, significantly to alter one's own position in the pecking order. One might have a good job, and have built an expensive house in the town's most sought-after locality, but one remains, more or less, the person one started out as. Appearances mean everything, and yet appearance means little or nothing. The social niceties that apply elsewhere carry no writ. You are given a role and a place in the maternity ward, and retain it throughout your life. If, for example, our two notional citizens, meeting in the street, come from the opposite ends of the town's spectrum of significance, but on this occasion happen to be dressed in precisely the same manner, and to a neutral outsider appear to be similar in every respect of their outward manifestation, then this will have precisely the opposite significance to the townspeople's understanding of themselves. Either the person from the better part of the town is dressing down, or the other is dressing up, and in either case the conclusions to be drawn will be to the disadvantage of the person who has attempted to interfere, by cosmetic means, with his place in the natural order of things.

Regardless of how many people are present, the process is the same. If one were to take, say, five people from various parts and backgrounds in such a town and, having dosed them with some form of truth serum, ask each of them to draw up a list placing themselves and the other four in the correct order of their 'importance' in the town, all five lists would be the same. Deep down, everybody knows where they stand.

Perhaps somewhere, in some secret place in the heaven or hell of such towns, there is a list showing the precise order of importance of every citizen who had ever lived in them. If we who grew up in such places were to be honest, this would not surprise us.

Clearly, segregation at this level is highly refined, though it has its cruder elements. Address, for example, is of primary importance, and it was all but impossible to alter the significance of where you lived. The social spectrum of the town of Castlerea was defined by Knockroe at the top end and Church Road at the other. The fact that these roads were connected at right angles to each other was of absolutely no consequence. The important factor was that the people of Knockroe owned their own houses, while the people of Church Road did not. In later years, when the town's expansion would lead to housing developments between the two roads, the inhabitants of these would jump down your throat at the merest suggestion that their new address was associated with Church Road by anything other than an accident of geography.

The other parts of the town came somewhere in between, with the main arterial thoroughfares of Main Street and Patrick Street occupying the centre. Our family lived on Main Street.

The individual's place in this pecking order was all but immutable, and his politics was an essential part of it. You grew up in the consciousness that your family was a 'Fianna Fáil family' or, as in our case, a 'Fine Gael family'. This did not have to mean that your family was particularly interested in politics, in the wider sense of the word, or indeed that politics, as such, ever entered the same consciousness wherein resided this awareness of where one's loyalties lay. Politics existed at different levels. There was a level of political activity in the town – people who took an active part in the organisation of one or other of the two main parties – but this, although related, was of a different order. Like the Church, which had its priests, sacristan and altar boys, so the political parties had their activists. These were the local guardians of the party's soul. But the spirit of the party in the constituency resided within the hearts of the people themselves, the people who had been 'born into' the party, most of whom were neither activists nor members of the party in question. You did not simply 'belong' to Fine Gael; you 'were' Fine Gael.

And as with the Church, it was possible to be aligned with a party without approving of the people with whom the spirit of that party was entrusted locally. People who became active in one of the two parties (there *were* only two parties) were not necessarily more devout than the average supporter, nor did they achieve levels of authority within the local organisation on the basis of popularity. They had become involved as a way of holding their own against the sometimes intolerable weight of the community, not in the sense that they could affect the quality or course of life in the town by their participation in politics, but in the sense that, by being engaged in politics, they created a reinforced shell around themselves and their families. When you took on a Fianna Fáiler, you took on not just the individual, but the entire party and all its mysterious works and ways. Generally speaking, those who became active in Fine Gael were people on the make locally, the kind of people who were 'stuck in everything' – from the dramatic society to the Legion of Mary – the kind of people who like ordering others around. They tended to come from the upper echelons of the town's hierarchy – shopkeepers, solicitors and the like – whereas the Fianna Fáilers usually were people with no great claims or pretensions who were simply chancing their arms. People whose job or social position gave them no right to speak out of turn could obtain this right by joining Fianna Fáil: in the sacred sanctuary of the party rooms, a postman or roadsweeper could take his turn to speak without having to bow to the lawyer or the draper's son. In either party, the character or calibre of the local activists would have little or no bearing on the strength of support for the party within the constituency. This was given or withdrawn for altogether more mystical reasons.

The town of Castlerea was run – in as far as it was 'run' at all – in a manner not in the least related to democracy. The town had grown up around the estate of the Sandfords, the local landlords, and had the benefit of a considerable area of demesne surrounding it, through which flowed the river Francis, a tributary of the nearby Suck. The lands around the river had some beautiful walks and ornamental gardens, all of which were maintained and overseen by a body called the Town Trust. This had been founded in the early years of the century, after the Sandford family had pulled out of Castlerea. Following their departure, the elders of the town had formed the Trust to administer the affairs of the estate. Householders in the town were canvassed to support the Trust by putting up their homes as security for the estate. About half agreed to do this.

Soon the estate was prospering again under its new ownership. Alas, if the householders had imagined that the departure of the Sandfords would mean a greater involvement for themselves in the running of the civic affairs of the town, they were greatly mistaken. In theory, the land of the estate belonged to ordinary inhabitants of the town, but in practice it was administered as though it belonged to the town's merchant and professional classes. The townspeople, even those who stood to lose their homes if the estate got into difficulty, were not consulted.

The Town Trust consisted of a handful of Castlerea's leading shopkeepers and professional people, who met regularly to discuss the administration of the demesne. They even had two employees – a secretary and a gardener. When a member of the Trust died, he or she was replaced by another shopkeeper, doctor or suchlike, who was co-opted onto the Trust by the other members. This situation continues to the present day.

At no time were the townspeople either consulted about the Trust's stewardship of the demesne or asked for an opinion on the profile of the Trust's membership. Its meetings were not open to the public, and the Trust did not issue reports of its activities. There were vague mutterings locally about one or two of its more dubious decisions – the sale of tracts of land for housing development, for example, or its refusal to allow the local soccer club to develop its ground in the demesne – but nobody ever managed to care sufficiently to object formally, or even to have arrived at the imaginative connection between the body, its title, and the fact that the rightful ownership of the demesne was vested in the community as a whole.

One of the few people ever to stand up to the Trust was my father, who, as the owner of a house on the town's Main Street, qualified as one of the estate's legal owners. As such, he was entitled to a shed in the yard of the Sandford house in the demesne, known locally as 'the Castle'.

In the late 1950s, wishing to avail himself of this entitlement, he applied to the Trust for permission to put his turf in one of the sheds in the Castle yard. He was refused. He learned from a renegade source on the Trust that they planned to sell off the Castle to the GAA as the site of a new football ground. My father, apart from the issue of the shed, was scandalised at the notion that they could consider demolishing a piece of local history to create space for a football field. He decided to take them on.

The chairmanship of the Town Trust fell by tradition to the local parish priest. The current incumbent was Canon Duignan, a cheerful, avuncular man whose stewardship of his local flock lacked any of the high-handedness or petty oppressiveness of many clerics of the time. He did not visit the homes of the better-off, as did many of his cloth, but was a benign, genial figure, genuinely loved by his people. A shy man, who kept himself to himself, Canon Duignan seemed to enjoy immensely the idea of discomfiting his parishioners. He could be seen most afternoons, walking in the demesne, waddling along with his dog and his umbrella. He knew the names of all the local children and enjoyed teasing them. As you approached him on the path, he would mischievously block your way; when you moved to avoid him, he would shift direction, trying to bring about a collision. When, finally, he had stalemated you to a standstill, he would stare at you and shake his head. 'Tsk, tsk, tsk,' he would say. As he did so, he would bring his umbrella down on your foot, pressing hard until you flinched. Then he might give you thrupence to buy some chewing gum.

The Canon hated the Town Trust and never went to its meetings. Because there was no discussion of the Trust's activities, nobody asked him why, but the chairman's chair remained vacant at each meeting for the duration of his pastorship. When the Trust turned down my father's application for a shed, he took his case to the Canon. The Canon listened, nodded, going 'Tsk, tsk, tsk' all the while, and told my father that he would look after it. During the next meeting of the Trust, the members were surprised by a loud banging on the door of their meeting room. It was the Canon hammering with the handle of his umbrella. He walked into the room and said, 'I want Tom Waters to have his shed in the Castle.' Then he turned and walked out.

The Canon's word was law. My father got his shed. But his tenancy was short-lived. One day, after a prolonged spell of heavy rain, he arrived at the Castle to find that the roof had been taken off and his turf had become saturated with rainwater. I remember shortly afterwards sitting with him at home while the explosions of the demolition contractors reduced the Castle to a pile of rubble. Each blast seemed to speak to us of who we were and where we stood in the town.

There was no line at which you could say that religion ended and politics began. Historians and sociologists often attempt to analyse the nature of support for the two main political parties in rural Ireland. In doing so they talk a great deal about 'civil war politics', implying that an understanding of what this means will allow the nature of modern politics to be understood. Nothing could be further from the truth.

For most people in rural Ireland, political allegiance is a matter of faith, not of belief. It is the allegiance itself, rather than the cause, that is important. The divide of Irish politics, Fine Gael versus Fianna Fáil, has its roots in the civil war, but it is the divide itself, rather than the war, that is the significant element. The important thing was to give your allegiance to the side you were born into, and maintain its integrity by opposing the other. It is not sufficient simply to support whatever side you yourself are aligned with; you must also attack, vilify and pour scorn on the other. Most people of my generation were brought up to know almost nothing, apart from a few slogans, of the civil war, but the schism it created continues to divide us cleanly, just as it would if we had been present ourselves. Most of us were given little or no education in the history of the divide that helped to define ourselves and so much of our public lives. Our knowledge and awareness of it came to us in fragments, little scraps of half-remembered stories, slogans and prejudices.

Not that any of this prevented us from throwing around

these slogans, with passion and vehemence. I had – still have – a few slogans of my own.

I gained whatever knowledge of politics I have in much the same way as I learned about television. We did not have a television set when I was growing up – or for a long time afterwards. My father thought it a bad influence, and anyway we had no electricity in the house until I was ten. But not having television was fatal to one's image and standing in school. Television programmes like *Batman*, *Get Smart* and *The Man from U.N.C.L.E.* accounted for most of the conversation that took place in the classroom and playground. Each morning I would listen carefully to accounts of incidents from the previous night's television programmes, memorise the details and then begin to talk about them as though I had seen them myself. I had learned all the slogans and the sound effects. 'Would you believe . . . ?' 'Holy cow!', 'Holy fire escape!', 'Pow!', 'Bop' and 'Thud!' Now I was Batman, now Robin, now the Joker, now Maxwell Smart. If you saw me jumping from behind cars on the way from school, you might have muttered impatiently to yourself, 'There's that horrible Waters boy, larking around': you would have been wrong. I was, in fact, Illya Kuryakin and was fearlessly engaged in a deeply personal struggle against the forces of the international crime syndicate, THRUSH. To this day, I have never in my life seen an episode of *The Man from U.N.C.L.E.*

This was the way we became aware of politics. I did not learn about politics; I soaked them up. I was 'born into' Fine Gael – I 'was' Fine Gael. 'I'm Fine Gael,' I can hear myself saying, still in short trousers. The Man from F.I.N.E. G.A.E.L. When T. F. O'Higgins was pipped for the presidency by Eamon de Valera in 1966, I cried for a day.

It was many years before this began to strike me as being in any way ludicrous, the idea of an eleven-year-old son of a County Roscommon mailcar driver bawling his eyes out on behalf of a leading member of the Irish judicial establishment. For a long time afterwards, my father would tease me about this: 'You've changed your tune. I remember when you cried for Tom O'Higgins.'

At no time did my father take me aside and explain to me the facts of Irish political life, but I took my politics from him all the same. My father was in a fairly unusual position locally in that he knew pretty well what the civil war was about. In 1922 he had been a teenager and from time to time would speak sparingly of the horror of the war. He blamed de Valera for 'setting brother against brother', and despised Fianna Fáilers on this account, not so much for their 'part' in the war itself, but because of their lack of shame on account of it.

I heard the slogans throughout my childhood without being particularly aware of what they signified. They were rooted in the civil war, and yet had very little to do with the reality of it; they were the slogans of one side or the other. History was what you needed it to be; it always is. There's even an axiom to this effect. History is written by the winners; except that, in our case, we had two versions of history – one written by the winners and the other by the losers. Each side believed that the other had lost. The two versions existed side by side in the streets of Ireland, sometimes in the same bed. Few could remember why they were on one side rather than the other, any more than they could say why they had been born male rather than female, or female rather than male.

From time to time one might be struck by the absurdity,

or even the sheer unfairness of it all. It would occasionally occur to me that I had never been given a choice in the matter of my 'politics', and that, moreover, as a result of this, I was, more often than not, on the losing side. Throughout my childhood and early teens, Fianna Fáil was in government. The president was a Fianna Fáiler. In my class at school, as indeed in every other domain, I was in the minority, the losing minority, and inevitably was the butt of much triumphalist Fianna Fáil humour. In a flash, a mixture of guilt and exhilaration, it would sometimes occur to me that I could fix this by simply changing sides.

One such moment occurred during the closing days of the 1966 presidential election. On my way to school one morning, a car covered with de Valera posters and stickers drove up Main Street, the loudhailer exhorting the populace to come out and support Dev. As he drove, the driver casually scattered leaflets behind him on the road. When he had gone on a little, I ran into the road and picked up as many as I could, jamming them into my schoolbag. They were colourful leaflets, with green and orange slogans and a picture of a smiling Dev. Our crowd did not stretch to leaflets like this; we had to make do with staid, black-and-white handout sheets with a sour photograph of T. F. O'Higgins. On my way into school I decided that I would change sides, that I would distribute the leaflets to my classmates as though I had been a Fianna Fáiler all my life – which from that day onwards I decided to become.

When I began to give out the leaflets, however, I realised that this might not be as easy as I had anticipated. The Fianna Fáilers appeared to find the new situation quite acceptable: few of them remarked on my change of allegiance, and I was not at all certain that it had been widely noticed. But it did not escape the notice of a few of my erstwhile Blueshirt colleagues. They did not approve. One boy in particular was outraged by my treachery. He grabbed the bundle of Dev leaflets and, despite my tearful protestations, tore them to pieces in front of the entire class. What I did notice was that neither Fianna Fáil nor Fine Gael supporters rushed to my aid. I was now the butt of both, a laughing stock. That would be the last time for many years that I would attempt to change sides.

3

The Democratic God

Years afterwards, when I began to learn something of de
Valera, I would come to regard my father's hostility to
him as rather odd. No one I have ever met conformed to
de Valera's notion of the ideal Irishman as did my father.
He shared de Valera's belief in the value of self-sufficiency
generated by hard work. This view was founded not on
xenophobia but on a profound belief, based on personal
experience, that self-reliance was the only sure way of
ensuring real prosperity and true independence. This
philosophy was inextricably bound up with my father's
religious outlook: he believed in the notion of the land as
the source of life, and that this connection was miraculous,
mysterious, rather than scientific reality. He was one of
the most genuinely religious people I have ever known. He
believed that the Earth was the custodian of a set of values
that were immutable, an energy that would serve mankind
well so long as we respected it as deriving from a higher
intelligence, and an equilibrium that we would attempt to
cheat or disturb at our peril. He was a devout Catholic,
saying the rosary every night, and visiting the church two

or three times a week, when he had finished his day's work, to do the Stations of the Cross and light candles.

My father did not think of the Church as being in the least an oppressive force; on the contrary, he regarded it as being on his side against the oppressiveness of the hierarchy, the tribe. The Canon was the ultimate and infinitely just dispenser of God's mercy and justice; the Almighty he represented seemed to be something of a social democrat. This undoubtedly played a big part in the fact that, although my father disagreed with de Valera about practically everything else, he always maintained that if Dev got one thing right in his life it was the 1937 Constitution. 'A Catholic Constitution for a Catholic people,' he would say in the midst of debates about the separation of Church and State, 'and what's wrong with that?' People of his generation were genuinely puzzled by discussion of the Catholic Church which characterised it as a monolithic institution; they saw the Church as a body of individuals, some of whom were good, and some, as in the world at large, who were not so good.

Given his professed abhorrence of its chief architect, my father's absolute fealty to the 1937 Constitution often struck me as absurd; but for him there was no contradiction. He respected the integrity of de Valera's attempt to regulate the affairs of the fledgling state, and never missed an opportunity to defend it. To my certain knowledge, he opposed every single attempt to introduce amendments to the Constitution, including the 'Right to Life' amendment of 1983. He did so not on moral, religious or political grounds, but because he believed that the Constitution would be undermined by such piecemeal alterations. The fact that de Valera was a 'bowsie' did not alter the quality of the Constitution, 'the only decent thing he ever did'. During a referendum campaign, my father was often to be found thumbing through his dog-eared *Dréacht Bhunreacht* in search of ammunition. For several years after the Right to Life amendment, he would tell of how, one Sunday at the Society for the Protection of the Unborn Child collection table outside the church, he had questioned a local 'pro-life' activist about the implications of the amendment, and would declare that 'she didn't know what she was talking about'.

I never heard my father raise his voice, and yet his quiet word was law. He never in my hearing, or that I am otherwise aware of, used a word stronger than 'bowsie' or 'louser'. He had been fifty at the time I was born, and so was a generation older than the fathers of most of my friends, a sort of father and grandfather all rolled into one. As a boy, I felt that there was nothing he did not understand, and there are times still when I feel I was more right than wrong about this. Many times when I ran into trouble with an algebraic problem at the kitchen table at night, he would scribble a few figures on a piece of paper and, by some complex process, get the answer that was at the back of the book. He could dismantle the most mysterious-looking gadgets and put them together again in perfect working order. Among the many machines he had collected were a number of gramophones, none of which ever worked for more than an hour or two. Every so often he would spread newspapers on the kitchen table and take one of them asunder, carefully cleaning and adjusting each part, his glasses perched on his forehead. When he had finished, he would put on a 78 record and, for a brief while, the machine would function as it had been intended to. And when the voice of John McCormack or Bridie Gallagher emerged from the machine, it was as though its art was the product solely of my father's genius, as though it was in some basic way connected to the grease on his fingers, the tools strewn all around him, the perspiration fogging up the glasses on his forehead. But, the feat of magic achieved, the machine would be wrapped up again and put back in its box. There was work to be done.

He worked at least twice as hard as most other men. He got up at 4.30 am, made his breakfast, and was waiting at the railway station by 5.30 for the arrival of the paper train. By six he would have delivered the morning papers to the shops in the town, and would go to the post office to fill his van with mail for delivery to the outlying sub-offices which came under the administrative control of the main office in Castlerea. From an early age I knew these off by heart: Loughglynn, Ballaghaderreen, Tibohine, Frenchpark, Ballinagare, Mantua, Elphin, Cloonyquin, Tulsk, Castleplunkett, Lisalway.

After this, about nine, he would deliver the morning papers to Ballintubber, Rath, Oran and Ballymoe. Then he would come home, have his breakfast proper, and head off to meet the midday train. From there he would set off again to Ballaghaderreen to deliver the second post. He worked more or less continuously throughout the day, finishing usually about 7.30 pm when he completed the day's collections of mail from the sub-post offices. He did this six days a week for over fifty years, working right up to his late seventies. Only then did he begin to show signs of weakening under the heavy mailbags, which he would fling across his shoulder as though they were no heavier than his coat.

His coat was, after perhaps his grandad glasses, the first thing you noticed about him. I do not think that de Valera fully appreciated the concept of 'frugal comfort', for as far as I am aware he never met my father or got to see his coat. When, in my teens, and in the vain and pompous manner of teenagers, I became conscious of such things, I would feel embarrassed by my father's lack of concern about his appearance, but as a boy I had only admiring eyes for his perverseness. He had several coats, just as he had several suits, several shirts, and even a second pair of boots. But he wore only two coats: one on Sundays and one on weekdays.

His weekday coat was invariably ripped and tattered, with strips of cloth and lengths of thread hanging off it at various angles. The pockets bulged with the many mysterious objects he collected and carried around with him at all times. When the contents of his pockets burst out through the bottom, he would tie the bottoms up with string; if the contents burst out again, he would give in and spend a Sunday at the kitchen table sorting through the pile of wrenches, screwdrivers, pliers, flashlights, balls of thread, penknives, keys, compasses, old washers, lengths of wire and other assorted curiosities that he had picked up over the previous few months, reluctantly eliminating those items that were not essential. If you did not know him, you might get to thinking that he did not like new things. But the truth was that he loved new things and hated to see them grow old. So he would wear a coat until it practically fell off his back, and drive vans that no one but himself was able to start.

He had a room in the front of the house which he called the 'shop', in which he kept all his tools. It was full to the ceiling of boxes packed with every conceivable type of tool for every imaginable trade or job. There was practically nothing in the line of carpentry, plastering, bricklaying, joinery – any kind of work with the hands – that he could not do. He resisted any attempt to have the room emptied for use as a sitting room. 'That is my life in there,' he would say, and pursuit of the issue led to a silence that might last for days.

When he died, in the summer of 1989, I knew that the funeral would not be over until we had removed every last hammer, every last nail, from the boxes in that room, taken them out of the house and allowed their lives to begin, just as we had taken my father himself down the stairs and put him in a box when his life was ended. We held an auction to which tradesmen from miles around came, to buy the dozens of hammers, saws, wrenches, drills, planes, chisels – about 4,000 lots in all, most of them still in their wrappers, and many swaddled carefully in newspaper and tied with twine. In some cases the newspapers dated back a quarter of a century.

My father was uncomfortable with the tribe, politely scorned its hierarchy and rejected any of its attempts to include him. He kept himself to himself, and spoke with the same politeness and respect to the town's biggest shopkeeper as he did to John Carr, the chimney sweep, with his burden of brushes and his blackened face.

Carr had his own way of dealing with the town. A small, stooped man of indeterminable age, he stalked through the town as though it did not exist, his brushes over his shoulder, from time to time spitting aimlessly and indifferently on the ground.

Between jobs, he would hide his brushes under the

bridge in the middle of town and disappear into Stephen Mannion's, the darkest and most forbidding pub in the street. For everyone in the town, whether they admitted as much or not, John Carr represented one extreme of the unwritten hierarchy. Because at that time he was the only chimney sweep in Castlerea, they allowed him reluctantly into their homes. When he had finished his work, they swept him out with the soot. Hardly anybody in the town treated Carr as an equal. He was a joke figure, a cartoon, a necessary nobody who did a dirty job.

I only ever saw John Carr talk seriously to children, and when he came to clean our chimneys I would sometimes ask him questions. He would reply, too, and not in the manner that his caricature persona suggested, but kindly, intelligently and humorously. In the street, in the grown-up world of the town, he greeted everybody he met with the same high-pitched, staccato phrase: 'Up Dev!' In this phrase was couched his entire public being. It was delivered with a mixture of seriousness and irony which nobody could penetrate. It was his protection against the world of the town and obviated the need for more detailed communication. Some people would laugh and reply in like manner. 'Up Dev! Good man, John!' Others would simply ignore him, unless they happened to be in imminent need of his services.

But I noticed that my father always greeted him with a 'Hello, John', and that Carr would reply, as he did to almost nobody else, without the mandatory 'Up Dev!'

'Hello, John.'

'Hello, Tom.'

They had in common, not just tattered coats, but the

fact that, however little else they shared, they were both outsiders in the town of Castlerea.

My father displayed a total indifference to the views that other people might hold of him. His life was an expression of fundamental imperatives, values that had to be practised and observed rather than merely articulated. Once he bought a farm from a family of three elderly people, two brothers and a sister, near Loughglynn village. In their sixties, they were still a few years younger than he was, and were unhappy to have to sell the farm on which they had lived all their lives. He visited them at home to shake hands on the deal. Sitting there, drinking tea, he sensed a deep unhappiness among the three people.

'Where will ye go?' he asked casually.

They had no place to go except the county home, they said. They had to sell to pay off the bank, but they hated leaving their home place. 'There's no need for ye to leave,' my father said. He told them that he would buy the farm, but they could remain in possession as long as any one of them was alive. 'And don't be in any hurry to die, let ye. If ye live another fifty years, then more luck to ye.'

As it happened, all three of them predeceased him, and finally we got to see the house and farm my father had spoken of for so long. It was a beautiful cottage on forty acres. I made the mistake of believing that it was his intention to retire there, and spent a couple of summers painting and decorating the house. But, though he continued to pay a vague lip-service to the idea, he warded off any suggestion of going to live there. I know now that, like the hammers and chisels in the 'shop' at home, the land he had bought was not intended for use in this world or lifetime. His frugality led inevitably to rumours that he was a 'millionaire', and 'eccentric' with it. For a time I even believed this myself. The truth, however, was that he had scrimped and saved for years to put together the makings of a life he would never live, a life that would be, in fact, unlivable, an illusory future held out by the rhetoric of the time meeting his own innermost aspirations. His small farms – 'Lynch's', 'Corcorans' and 'the Pope's', were their official titles – were stored up for the time when his life could begin. He had drawn a line in the earth of his future which he had no hope, and I now know, no intention, of ever reaching.

Only by being 'eccentric' could you place yourself outside the tribe. Because my father possessed the characteristic of not caring, he was regarded as an eccentric. One thing that contributed to his reputation in this regard was that he was a notoriously slow driver. I do not know whether he had always been a slow driver, but he had long since been one on principle. There were a few people around town whom he had taught to drive, and they too were slow drivers. As with his manner of dress, this became, when I grew into my teens, a source of some embarrassment, but to a child it was a cause only of wonder. He would cruise cheerfully along the road at speeds rarely exceeding twenty miles per hour. From time to time we might be overtaken by someone in a big, shiny new car, blowing for the road. 'See that bowsie,' my father would say with disgust. 'I knew that crowd when they had nothing but an ass and a bad cart.'

My father's vans, like his coats, always seemed on the point of disintegration. For years he drove a Thames 800 minibus, which went, literally, from week to week. He would work and drive all week and on Sunday would take the engine apart, lying black-faced on his back on the road under the engine, while I or one of my three sisters handed in the appropriate spanner or did duty by pumping the brake pedal.

As with his coats and suits, his insistence upon maintaining the old van until it fell away from under him seemed to derive from a philosophical outlook rather than necessity. In the archway of the house across the road, where we had been born and had lived until the mid-sixties, my father kept two or three other vans, which he used for spare parts, but which were in infinitely better condition than the one he was driving. For years I argued with him that it would be more economical to buy and maintain a new van. He did not agree but, even if he did, it would not have mattered. A mechanic by trade and training, he had driven cars and lorries from his teens, and was scornful of people who drove cars but knew nothing of the mysteries of how they worked. He himself liked to be in control of the machine, to be in touch with the source of the power that propelled it.

If the Thames 800 started at the first turn on Monday morning, he wanted it to be because he had spent most of Sunday tuning and nursing it, and not because people he had never met had put it together efficiently in a factory. To him a van was closer to an animal than to a machine. If you looked after it, it would remain your best friend; if you neglected it, it would sit down and refuse to get up. He enjoyed the idea of the van being just a whisker away from a total crock. That way, it was part of him, part of the meaning of his life.

It is not possible to exaggerate. The van was held together with pieces of string and rope. Three of the four hinges on the back doors were broken, as was the lock and the handle. The doors were kept in place by a long rope tied to the glove compartment in the dashboard. Another rope secured the front passenger door. Both the driver's and front-seat passenger's doors had parted company from one or other of their hinges and had come adrift, leaving a good four or five inches of space between door and jamb, and turning the van into an icebox in winter. I do not recall any van of my father's ever having a heater. The floor of the van had long since rotted from weather and age, and he had patched it up with sheets of tin and plywood.

In addition to delivering mail and newspapers, my father also had a hackney licence; this allowed him to carry passengers. On some of the routes he covered there was no public transport and so the mailcar also functioned as a sort of bus service. On the midday run to Ballaghaderreen, for instance, and particularly on Thursdays and Fridays, he might have up to twenty passengers in the van. The seats had been removed from the back of the van, and so the clientele sat on every available flat surface: the engine cover between the two front seats, wooden boxes, the two spare wheels (my father always carried two spare wheels, being deeply pessimistic about punctures), even on the floor.

Most of his passengers were small farmers and their families from the villages and townlands along the Loughglynn/Ballaghaderreen road. Some were going in to collect pensions or dole money, others to shop; others were going in for a day's drinking. For all of them the journey in and out was an essential part of their social life. It was the only time that many of them met during the week, the one opportunity to talk to people outside their own households for anything more than a businesslike few moments. It was not a long journey – Ballaghaderreen was only twelve miles from Castlerea and less than six from Loughglynn – but because my father was such a slow driver, there was plenty of time to talk.

I have often heard it pointed out locally that my father's job was like the stagecoach driver's. I have used the analogy myself, and it is to some extent a good one. On Saturdays or during school holidays, I helped out on the run. My role was to let the passengers in and out through the middle door, which, naturally, had no handle. When someone wanted to get in or out, I had to untie the rope that held shut the front passenger door, take a large screwdriver from under the seat and open the door by literally picking the lock. I would pull out the wooden box, which was kept under the back seat for use as a step, and help the passenger out onto the road. If they had any large parcels, or perhaps a bicycle or bag of coal, I would have to untie the rope that tied the back doors to the dashboard. You might say that I rode shotgun.

But Tom Waters was much more than the stagecoach driver, and the Thames van was much more than a surrogate for public transport. The atmosphere in the van was somewhere between a public house and a theatre. There was no beer, but there was plenty of drama. All present were both performers and audience. The Thames 800, on Thursdays and Fridays, was the nearest they came to a social occasion in which men and women, neighbours and their children sat together and talked in more or less egalitarian surroundings. (There were, of course, innumerable pubs in the area: two in Loughglynn and practically one for every two houses in Ballaghaderreen.

But women – certainly not these women – did not go into pubs.)

On any one day, the number of people in the van might be counted as a handful, but the mailcar's influence in the locality radiated far beyond that number. People discussed what had been said in the van: 'What about Harry?', 'Did you hear what Tom said to Frank?', 'Frank fairly took the rise out of Mary Kate!' My father was the chairman and master of ceremonies, the Ceann Comhairle and referee, the Brian Farrell and John Bowman of the Thames 800. He prodded and adjudicated, prompted and teased. The respect they accorded him went beyond the fact that he was the driver, and therefore the host.

He was older than most of them. They admired his mildness, his easy wisdom, his sense of humour, his knowledge of history and the affairs of the world. He had a ready grasp of strange concepts like the New Departure, the Tariff Commission, and the First Programme for Economic Expansion. Most of what he knew had been learned from the newspapers; he rarely had time to read books, although he had a roomful of assorted volumes, ranging from Shakespeare to popular mechanics, which he had accumulated in his youth. He had a dog-eared draft version of *Bunreacht na hÉireann*, which he appeared to have learned by heart. His regular passengers looked upon him as the fount of all political wisdom, and treated his every utterance of opinion with a respect approaching reverence.

Most of the people we carried were supporters of Fianna Fáil. This was not an intellectual position; it was a condition that permeated every fibre of their beings. They did not support Fianna Fáil because of its policies, or because it was in government at the time. They supported Fianna Fáil, as far as one could make out, because they were Fianna Fáilers. It was in the Thames that I learned what Fianna Fáilers looked like. I noticed, too, that they looked a lot like me. They were like me, and like my father as well. These were his people; he was at ease with them and they with him. He knew them all intimately and was acquainted with the personal circumstances and family history of each one of them.

He differed from them only on politics, and then only in terms of allegiance. So great was his affinity with Fianna Fáilers that I could never completely understand how he had sustained his allegiance to Fine Gael. He seemed to sit more easily with the smallholders we met on the Ballaghaderreen run than with the ragbag of small-time shopkeepers and on-the-make professional classes who made up the core of Fine Gael's support in Castlerea. His support for Fine Gael was based largely, it seemed to me, on his regard for James Dillon, who owned a shop in Ballaghaderreen. Dillon, who had been leader of Fine Gael up to 1965, was an almost other-worldly figure in local politics, an independent-minded man who in his time had fought twelve general elections, and had a reputation for putting strong personal principles before party considerations. Despite the social distance that existed between Dillon, a barrister, farmer and leading member of the merchant classes, and the people of Ballaghaderreen, Fine Gael under his leadership was something to which my father had no difficulty in subscribing.

When Dillon was succeeded by Liam Cosgrave, a rather dull but equally principled politician, whose family name had deep Fine Gael associations, my father continued to be loyal to the party. Moreover, he had been personally friendly with James Burke, the local Fine Gael TD from Tulsk, who had served in thc Dáil between 1954 and his sudden death in 1964. Afterwards my father continued to support Burke's wife, Joan, who was elected in the subsequent by-election, and represented Fine Gael in the Dáil until 1981.

But to a large extent these considerations were secondary. Party leadership or personnel, much less party policy in the mundane and everyday sense, had very little to do with allegiance.

Politics was at once deeply embedded in the culture of the place and the time, and yet curiously removed from it. Politicians, national or local, were shadowy figures, who came and went in hurries and flurries, surrounded by aides and local activist minders who shielded them from the public at large. The connection between the culture of this form of politics and the way the country was run and organised had never been registered. Politics had no visible impact on the surrounding landscape, or on the lives of the people. Survival, which was really all that mattered, depended on going on as you had always done. Each morning you got up and struggled against the day. The notion that this lot might in any way be improved by the actions of politicians was so ludicrous that it was never even discussed. Issues, policies, initiatives, which the politicians would bring forward from time to time, were minutely dissected and discussed, in the Thames 800 as elsewhere. Yet there was a clear though unspoken understanding that it was not the content of such things that mattered, but their potential for scoring points against the other side. They were the balls that would be thrown into the game: decentralisation, draining the Shannon, joining the Common Market.

Even when the politicians indulged in rhetoric, suggesting that such initiatives might have a direct and beneficial impact on the lives of the very people from whom they obtained the political lifeblood of support, this was never regarded as more than a necessary gambit by which to gain an advantage for 'our' side.

The real cause of the division that defined Irish politics derived from altogether different sources. In my father's case, his all-consuming interest in politics was propelled in the main by his fierce, passionate suspicion of de Valera. Yet in the 1970s, a number of things occurred that served, if not to dilute this passion, at least to redirect it.

4

The Mohair Suit

To put it simply: up until the very late seventies, by which time I was well into my twenties, my politics were defined by my father in precisely the same way as his had been defined by de Valera. One could put it even more strongly: my father defined my politics in the same way that Dev had defined the nation's up to his death and beyond. As a child I had accepted my father's word as writ, yet as I grew up I rebelled against him, thought him old-fashioned, backward-looking. In him I had someone to both measure myself against and to rebel against when the time came. Although, so to speak, we were on the other side of the family, I was Dev's political grandson.

But it would be a mistake to imagine that politics impinged very much upon what might be described loosely as our consciousness. Politicians were figures flitting across the screens of the television sets I would occasionally get to look at in the house of a friend or neighbour. They were grey and flavourless men, who appeared to run the country out of a sense of duty rather than with any real enthusiasm. Politicians were people of stature, people of distinction, people the rest of the population could look up to, as one might to an older brother or sister.

Some of them had unusual names. The Taoiseach was a man called Lemass, one of only two Lemasses in the phone book (the other was a judge). He had an openness about him that today would seem strange in a politician. Lemass did not live in fear of the electorate's judgement; he seemed to be able to take it or leave it. 'There are a great many times when I feel frustrated and exhausted,' he once said in an interview in the religious magazine, *The Word*, 'and where the prospect of walking out and leaving the whole thing behind me is terribly attractive. A President of one of the South American states did just this, didn't he? He took a boat for Europe and left everything behind him. I can understand this very well indeed.' In a strange way, the notion that the country was being run by someone who felt and thought just like the rest of us seemed very appealing. Politics is a matter of feeling, not knowledge.

A small minority have studied the life of Sean Lemass, and delivered verdicts on his contribution to Irish history. The great majority remember him only as a warm, fatherly figure who smoked a pipe and did not seem to be in love with power. Because he had been involved in the 1916 Rising, Lemass appeared to have an almost proprietorial sureness about the way he ran the country. 'If I wanted a house, I'd borrow to buy it,' he told an interviewer who queried his government's proclivity for borrowing. 'I wouldn't live in a tent till I had saved up the price of a house.'

Lemass spoke a language that reduced ideological conundrums to everyday terms. He seemed also to want to draw a line across the roadway to the past: 'We're moving into a new situation where the association with a political party is due to the intellectual decision of the individual, rarely prompted by the alignment of his father or grandfather. And of course this is going to alter the character of our parties and complicate the problem of party leadership.' My father did not support Lemass, but he did not dismiss him either. On the subject of Lemass, he remained silent and watchful.

Because of the influence of television and the cinema, the world revealed itself to my generation in images, one following on another, building up into a picture that deep down we assumed would have dramatic coherence when it was complete. We placed ourselves at the centre of this narrative, though we did not question or analyse the role we were supposed to be playing. On television, everything always had a beginning, a middle and an end. Life revealed itself in neat three-part packages. Act One: monkey climbs tree. Act Two: man shakes tree. Act Three: monkey comes down from tree. Everything came to him who waited. We picked up on the incandescent sense of optimism of our times, without knowing how this feeling was to be converted to our advantage.

We had free secondary education, and Donogh O'Malley's school buses brought us townies in contact with the sons and daughters of the small farmers from the hinterland of the town. We were on the road to somewhere, though we never stopped to ask our destination. There was, as the clichés had it, a 'sense of dynamism' in the country. The rising tide was raising all boats. It did not occur to us that this process might not include us, that the tide had discretionary powers. We were caught in the soap opera of the middle sixties; and the theme music had an upbeat rhythm, the plot would provide its own resolution. In a world tightly controlled by a rigid sense of hierarchy, we were given ideas above our station, but not the means by which to attain them.

It would be some years after I had left school, for example, before it would occur to me that, although a university education would have been essential to enable me and most of my school friends to accomplish our vaguely formed aspirations, the word 'university' was hardly ever mentioned in our hearing. In our class, a few of the boys from better-off backgrounds were given special coaching in the honours courses, unbeknownst to the rest of us. We had no way of knowing that we were to be squashed between the reality of our culture and origins and the misty mirage of our imagined futures.

Politicians were vague figures moving through the narrative. One of these was a man called Brian Lenihan, who had been a Fianna Fáil TD for the Roscommon constituency since 1961. In the sixties he was made, first, Minister for Justice, and then Minister for Education on the sudden death of Donogh O'Malley. His replacement of O'Malley, in retrospect, seems like a turning point in Irish politics. The two men were close friends, both members of what became known as The Men in the Mohair Suits, but there was a difference in the way the public perceived them. O'Malley was both loved and respected, Lenihan was merely loved. It was not just O'Malley's achievement in bringing in free secondary education and school transport, but also his age and the social chasm which still divided politicians of his generation from the ordinary citizens.

Like Lemass, O'Malley was a friendly yet distant man, a cross between a father figure and an avuncular teacher.

When he died suddenly in 1968, we were sent home from school; we walked back down the town through streets in which you could taste the sense of numbed loss. But Lenihan was a decade younger than O'Malley, and lacked that air of big-brotherly authority. It was hard to believe that he was a politician at all; he was one of us, and it did not seem quite right that one of us should be in such a senior position in the running of the country. He was chubby, jolly and a bit of a bluffer. People smiled when his name was mentioned.

Lenihan's role as a politician appeared to be in some way detached from his role in the running of the country. He was two different people: now the glad-handing politician in the constituency, now the man in the mohair suit. He was a hard-working constituency TD, as you had to be, holding regular clinics in the towns and villages of County Roscommon. The fact that he was a minister was an extra bonus. Going to him at one of his clinics was like going to confession to a bishop. In Dublin he was in with the In-crowd. His constituents in Roscommon viewed this aspect of Lenihan with sardonic detachment. The two roles were mutually dependent and yet could not be reconciled.

Every so often, usually during election campaigns, Lenihan would arrive in town in a flurry of black cars, loud hailers and much triumphalism among his local supporters. Word of mouth would bring the people onto the street.

Round about teatime one evening, in the middle of the 1973 general election campaign, the word went out that Lenihan, now Minister for Foreign Affairs, was about to begin speaking in the Market Square. The trickle of people leaving their houses rapidly became a flood, and by seven o'clock the Square was filled almost to capacity. The Minister was sighted. He was wearing a shiny blue suit, the likes of which nobody in the town had ever laid eyes upon. He was whisked away through the crowd to be refreshed, while the other, less important, speakers were delivering their speeches. The platform was the back of a lorry, on which had been arranged a row of light, tubular-steel chairs borrowed from the hotel across the street.

Brian Lenihan, I noticed even then, had an extra-ordinary way of speaking. His speeches flowed like a piece of music, building all the time. He invariably gave much the same speech, about the rising tide and the raising of boats, though he might occasionally alter the refrain, depending on the subtleties which he was adept at detecting in a gathered crowd. But it was not so much the content of the speech that mattered as the rhythms, the repetition of key phrases and the inexorable progress towards a devastating climax of hyperbole. But tonight, so transfixed was the crowd with the minister's suit, that they hardly noticed even the swelling rhythms of the speech.

When he had finished speaking, the minister raised his hands to accept the applause of his supporters and then made to sit down on one of the waiting, tubular chairs. Alas, instead of easing himself gingerly onto the chair, as a man of his considerable girth might have been advised to do, he plumped himself down, exhausted by his exertions. The chair gave way underneath him.

There followed a tremendous ripping sound, which brought down silence upon the assembled multitude. A mixture of anxiety and stifled amusement swept through the crowd, as though a teacher had let a fart and was waiting to see if anyone in the class would laugh. The word went around: the minister's mohair suit was torn. The arse had been taken out of it by the crude undergrowth of the steel chair. The minister was helped to his feet. He adjusted his clothing to protect his modesty as best he could. A tremor of suppressed laughter swept through the crowd. The minister approached the microphone. 'I hope,' he declared, 'that this doesn't mean I'm going to lose my seat in the Dáil.' The crowd broke into loud and uproarious laughter.

Within weeks, after a muddled and complacent campaign, Brian Lenihan had indeed lost his seat in the Dáil. The laughter that had greeted his unfortunate accident in the Market Square of Castlerea had been as coded as one of his own speeches. After 1973, Brian Lenihan moved his political base to Dublin, where eventually he would rebuild his political career and go on to re-establish himself centrestage in Irish politics.

In such ways did politicians and their people become connected and disconnected. At some point in the recent past, the thread of history had been broken, and the link lost between politics and what had once been their content: things like principles, historical events, ideas and beliefs. Instead, the culture of politics was connected in the people's imagination only with images and the rhetoric of buzzwords that summoned up the old, tribal allegiances.

Where once there had been an acute awareness of history and its trajectory, now there was but a narrative coherence provided by a loosely connected succession of images. Politicians no longer stood for things; they were merely on the same side as people who had once stood for things which, although more or less forgotten, defined the character of the divide between the two sides in the contest. Or they were on the other side.

5

The Morning After Optimism

I never really knew what people meant when they spoke of 'rural Ireland'. It is a Dublin term, at least one that is used by people addressing the rest of the country on radio and television programmes emanating from Dublin. What they usually intend to refer to is that part of the country which is not Dublin. Occasionally it is used to signify places outside the larger cities – Cork, Limerick, Galway – and sometimes even slightly smaller places such as Waterford and Sligo, which are then absorbed into the corollary, 'urban Ireland'.

Both places are crude inventions. When we were growing up, if we were asked to define rural Ireland, we would casually have mentioned those places in which there was a preponderance of trees and fields. Although Castlerea was, and still is, a town of just under 2,000 people, to us children it was a metropolis. I do not mean that we imagined it to be bigger than it was: we were all too conscious of its limitations. The point is that we were urbanites, with what we imagined was an urban sensibility. Country people were something quite different: oddly enough, they were people who lived in the country. We called them 'culchies', 'country mugs', or 'mulchies'. *We* were different: we were from the town. They called us 'townies', which we hated, and sneered that all we knew about spuds was to 'pale them and ate them', which cheered us considerably, since we had no desire whatever to know anything about spuds.

We grew up in the consciousness that we were where the action was, that our town was the centre of the universe. Most of the imagery our generation digested – from comics, television and the cinema – was the imagery of the city: Gotham City, Honolulu, San Francisco. The TV heroes we identified with were city people, and we identified with them to precisely the same extent as did our contemporaries in Dublin, Cork and Limerick. Our town might have had only a handful of streets, but it had most of the things that, in our eyes, constituted an urban sprawl. There were shops of almost every imaginable kind, public houses, cafés, a takeaway, several betting shops, a hotel, a dancehall, a cinema, and even a Protestant church.

The street of any town, almost regardless of how small, is both a world of its own and a way into another world. If you sit in a room in such a town and listen to the sounds of the street – the cars, sirens, horns, malfunctioning alarms, pneumatic drills, high-heeled shoes, shouts, all the assorted cacophony – it will strike you immediately that you are in a place that belongs at least as much to the universality of urban life as it does to its geographical location in the West of Ireland or wherever.

We had our first kisses in shoeshop doorways. The music we liked was rock music – Taste and the Stones – complex, challenging and strange, like the rhythm of the town, and so unlike the turgid dirges of what was appropriately called 'country' music, the music favoured by our country cousins, who lived less than a mile away in any direction. As teenagers, we sneeringly dismissed the music of the 'country mugs', the Country and Irish bands that played most Sunday nights in the Casino ballroom across the river, a few hundred yards from our house. Not for us Big Tom and the Mainliners, Gene Stuart and the Mighty Avons, Hugo Duncan and the Tall Men. We waited half the year for Horslips, Thin Lizzy, or The Freshmen. They provided music that was emblematic of our experience, though we could not say why.

Like Bernard Briggs and Roy of the Rovers, we played football in the street, and it was the street of a modern, urban, even industrial world (we even had, from time to time, a factory in the town). We had different accents from the country people: theirs were broader, thicker and flatter than ours. We did not live in the country: we lived in the Universal City. And this placed us right at the centre of the universe.

It was, of course, rather unsettling to be living so close to what was clearly the country. As a child, I would stand looking out of the rear skylight window of our house at the countryside spread far and wide around the town, and wonder at the way the view would jar with the sound of the street at the front.

The 'country', with all its strangenesses, was at any time only a few hundred yards away. When you walked out of our back door and kept going, within a minute you were in the middle of a vast area of waste ground, held in common by the residents of the street, which embraced all the furniture of a rural landscape. There were gardens overgrown with nettles and giant noxious weeds, an expanse of grass on which we played football or a neighbour jumped his racehorse, then a field into which the river Suck overflowed in winter, bringing the wonder of water to the bottom of our football pitch.

By the river bank we had felled a tree, fashioning a makeshift bridge, by which we gained access to an island: a vast and secret place, full of nooks and crannies, in which we built camps and waged war on rival tribes.

As a child I walked daily in this world, a world I knew to be connected with that of my aunt's farm in Cloonyquin, where we spent the three months of the summer holidays and which I could not get enough of. It, in turn, was linked with the world of my father's mailrun, and with the people who inhabited it.

But as we grew, we shut out this world. Unlike previous generations, we absorbed little of the language of the countryside – the names of plants and birds, for example, or the strange and wondrous working of nature's casual cycle. Many of us grew up to have almost a contempt for what was at best the womanly wonder of nature. We could not reconcile it with the bright lights of the town. Plugged in as we were to the Universal City, the country represented backwardness, thick accents and the past. We believed ourselves to be part of the thrusting, modern, forward-looking Ireland, which we had tasted on the wind.

Our world was a fragile illusion, but we managed to maintain it for most of the time. It was particularly difficult in our family, because my father was not a man to allow illusions to be fostered in his presence. He was an outsider, caring nothing for either the petty snobberies of the town or the flash promise of modernity. His tattered coat was part frugality and part statement. His heart lay with the countryside, where he had been born and where his soul, at least, intended to remain.

My father bought trees, which we reared in the back garden before planting them out on one of the farms in Loughglynn. He marked the spot, his brother Martin planted the trees, and I filled in the holes. He rammed our faces in the earth and rubbed them there till the earth was in our mouths. On Saturdays, for pocket money, I rode shotgun on the van, picking the lock to admit the impoverished smallholders whose soulmate he was. At his insistence I was forced to look beyond the town, to uncurl my nose from the scent of the turf smoke and the sweat of hard work. He brought us back to earth.

Yet not even this was sufficient preparation for the jolt that awaited us. We did not grow up wanting to be farmers, or mailcar drivers; we were born to grander things. If asked to say exactly what, we could not say. In the optimistic, forward-looking world where we lived, ambition and aspiration were everything.

In retrospect, it is possible to see that our ideas of betterment were vaguely tied in with the glamorous world of the city, with showbiz, soccer and stardom. Such imagery was all around us, and seemed to fit in with the political rhetoric of the time.

But if our ideas were of the future, our opportunities were firmly rooted in the past. Castlerea had all the imagery, rhythm and illusion of the modern streetscape, but it had none of the city's ability to look after its own. The only major employer in the town was the psychiatric hospital, and opportunities there were scarce enough even for those whose ambitions lay in that direction. In the seventies, a number of advance factories were built in the town, and from time to time a new firm, usually American, would move in, employ a handful of locals, operate for a year or two and then move out again as suddenly as it had arrived. Usually these were 'nut and bolt factories': the firm would transport the equivalent of a nut and a bolt from the USA, screw them together in its Castlerea operation, and then send them back to the mother country. When the government subsidies ran out, so did the factory, and the town went back to square one.

There were therefore few opportunities in the industrial sector locally, even for those who cared for the delicate work of screwing together nuts and bolts.

In lots of ways we were luckier than previous generations. We, at least, went to secondary school, to Mean Scoil Iosef Naofa in Patrick Street, which had been established in the 1940s by Mary O'Flanagan. Miss O'Flanagan, a radical and ferocious woman, was the niece of Father Michael O'Flanagan, the Republican Priest, whom Sean Lemass had dubbed the 'self-appointed Pope of the revolution', and to whose memory a bridge had been erected over the river Suck at the western end of the town. She was known locally as 'Mary O'.

Although the Sisters of Mercy catered for the girls, there had been no secondary school for boys in the town before the arrival of Mary O. As has been said so often of the work elsewhere of the Christian Brothers, Mary O provided a basic secondary education for many Castlerea boys, who otherwise would not have got one. But she could not fight the apartheid of economics or the unwavering hierarchy of the town. In the early days, before the advent of 'free' education, Mary O survived on the minuscule fees paid by parents. But when the boys of the better-off farmers and shopkeepers had completed the Inter Cert, they were shipped off to boarding school – to St Nathy's in Ballaghaderreen or to Summerhill College in Sligo. This prevented the expansion of the school in the early days, and insinuated a misplaced feeling of inferiority in the minds of the townspeople about the quality of the education on offer.

For myself and those of my contemporaries who had no option of going anywhere after the Inter, the possibility of attending university was never mooted. By this time I had decided that I wanted to be a journalist, but had only the vaguest notion of what I might have to do to achieve this. In the end, most of us did the basic Leaving Cert, taking the safe option of doing pass level in every subject. We arrived in the real world with the discovery that somewhere along the line we had been sold the pup of high hopes, but were now faced with altogether more modest horizons.

My father wanted me to study agriculture in the Regional Tech in Sligo. I was interviewed and gained a place, but something in me resisted what I suspected he was guiding me towards. I refused to go, and for several months not a word was exchanged between us. Eventually I got a job as a clerk with CIE. I have always suspected that my father used whatever political pull he possessed to secure it for me, our crowd being in power for a change. My first posting was in the railway station at Claremorris, mainly crosschecking despatches of bacon by rail from Claremorris Bacon Factory. It would be at least a year before I would begin to get over the shock. Whatever vague imaginings I might have had as a teenager about my future destiny, they did not include sorting through piles and piles of greasy invoices in search of stray bales of bacon, and taking abuse from a pig-voiced man in the bacon factory, as was now my daily lot.

Yet I was among the lucky ones: most of my classmates had simply gone to work in their fathers' farms or shops, or had set off for Dublin or London in search of work on the buildings. This was very far from our new gold dream.

I resolved to quit, but my father would not hear of it. How could I even think of leaving my lovely job, with its prospect of a good pension in forty-six years' time? I applied for other jobs on the sly, but with a singular lack of success. I wrote pathetic letters to newspapers, begging to be employed in any capacity that would allow me to work towards my goal. Some of the replies were even more pathetic: 'I have read your letter with interest and indeed a touch of sadness. We receive many such letters but, alas, we can seldom do much to help the aspiring journalist who is positioned as you are.'

It was a full four years before I made the break, landing a job preparing the news for a pirate radio station that had opened in Castlerea. After stints in Westport and Galway after Claremorris, I cashed in my CIE superannuation scheme and jumped ship. My father was beside himself, and an extended Cold War ensued. The situation was not helped by the fact that the radio station collapsed after three months. I went to Dublin, came back, joined a showband as a roadie, and finally, when my father became ill, returned to take over the stagecoach.

My father greeted this development with a mixture of disappointment and delight. Like most parents, he wanted his children to do better out of life than he had. On the other hand, he had a deep, almost spiritual, attachment to the mailrun, and was pleased that it was staying in the family.

I shared his ambivalence. He had brought me up as an outsider, but I lacked his innate tranquillity, his capacity for not caring. I had grown up in the expectation of transcending the provincialism of the small town, I had bought the rhetoric of the rising tide, I had even dipped my toe in its waters, but now I was definitively back to earth. I had woken up on the morning after optimism. The hierarchy, which demanded above all that nobody defy it, that each individual accept his or her fate and place, was pleased that I had seen the error of my ways.

In fact, I had also begun to write for *Hot Press*, a Dublin-based music magazine which had been in existence since the mid-seventies. During the week I drove the mailcar around the towns and townlands of west Roscommon; at the weekends I went to rock gigs and concerts in Sligo, Longford and Galway. The dream of the Universal City was still buried deep in my soul and would not be budged. I installed a radio-cassette player in my Hiace and blasted the roads of Aughaderry and Tibohine with Tom Waits and Elvis Costello.

This was the first half of the eighties, a time when the Irish psyche was in deep trauma. These were the years of the Abortion Amendment, Ann Lovett, GUBU and the Fianna Fáil leadership heaves, and the years when the name of one of our local TDs, Sean Doherty, became a byword for almost every kind of malaise to affect the Irish body politic.

As I drove around County Roscommon in the mornings listening to the radio, strange feelings began to possess me. The situation I found myself in, the places I went, the people I met, appeared utterly foreign and unexpected. In some ways I felt as though I had been dropped onto an alien planet, and yet the landscape was in almost every respect all too familiar. The radio pumped out sounds and voices from Dublin, a place with which I now knew I had been reared in total affinity. These voices stretched out across the midlands, across the 100-odd miles that separated us from the capital. But they, like me, might have been from another world. The voices on the radio seemed like the voices of a disappointed future hectoring away at an indigent and recalcitrant past. And I was the driver of the time machine that brought them face to face on the road to Ballaghaderreen.

6

Babyface and the Arms Trial

I cannot remember the precise time when my father began to support Fianna Fáil, but I assume that it was around the time Charles J. Haughey became party leader and Taoiseach, as we drew the last few gasps from the fag-end of the seventies.

Like a lot of people, like half the country, my father had long had a high degree of regard for Haughey. This was to some extent due to his fine record as a minister up to 1970, but even more so to the events in which Haughey became embroiled that year.

In my father's opinion, the ascent of Jack Lynch to the position of Fianna Fáil leader and Taoiseach had been a mistake, an aberration. Even though my father was a Fine Gaeler, he had long since reconciled himself to the notion that Fianna Fáil would be in power for most of the time within his likely lifetime, and as a result, had begun to take a more detached view. Initially this detachment did not mean a distancing of himself from Fine Gael, which in his view maintained the Holy Grail of principled and God-given leadership. But, having accepted the status quo, he began increasingly to apply himself to the way the infidel was carrying out its stewardship of the country. At first this took the form of asserting that any Fianna Fáil politician he admired 'should be in Fine Gael'. I had the feeling that this was his fervent wish in the case of Sean Lemass. But as time went on and de Valera became more blind and less visible, my father was able to see occasional good in Fianna Fáil.

Nonetheless, he had no time at all for Jack Lynch. This was not a hate affair to match that with which he had engaged himself with de Valera, but it was enough to be going on with. My father had little time for sport and was contemptuous of the fact that Lynch had come into politics as a result of his popularity as a GAA player. He did not regard Lynch as a proper politician and felt that Fianna Fáil's choice of him as leader represented a failure of nerve. Wherever there were two sides from which to choose, my father would align himself with one extreme or another. You could be one of us or one of them, but you could not be neutral. He had looked from George Colley to Charles Haughey and had made his choice. Fianna Fáil's choice of Lynch was to him a disgusting compromise.

In the years between 1966 and 1970, my father had felt that the mistake was not a fatal one: Lynch was at the helm, but was overshadowed by the performance of his ministers Donogh O'Malley, Kevin Boland and Charles Haughey. In due course, Haughey would inherit the shop. The things he admired in Haughey, oddly enough, were the same qualities he had admired in James Dillon: single-mindedness, authoritativeness and independent thinking, though in other respects the two men could hardly have been more different. For him, Lynch was none of these things. My father called him 'Babyface'.

The Arms Trial, which came out of the eruption of the Troubles in the North, both queered the pitch and galvanised his feelings on Haughey. This, I think, was an inevitable result of the kind of politics that had existed up to then: if there were two sides, you instinctively took one or the other, and it sucked you in. My father's feelings on the North, like those of many in the Republic, were confused; he related it directly to the civil war. He responded immediately and passionately on the side of the nationalists. His attitude to the events leading up to the Arms Trial was that, if Haughey indeed had been involved in importing arms for use by Catholics in the North, then this was no more than his duty as an Irishman and a member of the government of the Republic.

If Lynch had sent in the army, I think my father felt, we could all, once again, be on the same side. This was an emotional rather than a rational position, but it made sense in the context of his other beliefs. By standing by, and then by sacking, Haughey, thereby instigating the Arms Trial, Lynch not only confirmed my father's worst opinions about him, he also attempted to deny the past and yet failed to take his opportunity to transcend it. He created a new division: from now on, the division of loyalties would be no less passionate, but would become more and more complex.

Throughout the seventies, my father continued to support Fine Gael. He voted for them in 1973 and 1977. He had a deep respect for Liam Cosgrave. Any reservations he held about the 1973–77 coalition government were funnelled off in denouncing the Labour members of that administration. But his real passions became disengaged from what he now regarded as the unnatural and bogus division of Irish politics. There was no glory in Fine Gael being in government, when the opposition was represented by Babyface and his collection of compromise second-raters. These were not worthy opponents. Although my father maintained his interest in the cut and thrust of the political first division, his preoccupation was increasingly the approaching struggle for the soul of Fianna Fáil, and the re-emergence of Charlie Haughey.

This attitude was copperfastened in 1977 by the emergence of Garret FitzGerald as leader of Fine Gael. My father had had a high regard for FitzGerald in government under Liam Cosgrave, but did not regard him as leadership material. FitzGerald talked too much, and yet seemed to invest little substance or passion in the things he said. He had an impressive intelligence, but it seemed up to then to have been applied to things that had little relevance to the lives of the people he aspired to rule. He seemed anxious to impress us with his erudition and his grasp of figures, to dazzle us with his brilliance and then bask in our admiration. His rhetoric was powerful, but it lacked practicality. FitzGerald, my father felt, was making it up as he went along; he did not ring true. When the FitzGerald-inspired reorganisation of the party in Roscommon resulted in the departure of the sitting TD, Joan Burke, the die was cast. Fine Gael had changed hands, and my father felt free to pursue an interest in the fate of the Soldiers of Destiny.

7

The Discordant Drum

When I read much later what Marshall McLuhan had written about radio being 'utterly explosive' for particular sorts of communities, I knew immediately and exactly what he meant, and the sort of people he was talking about. 'For tribal peoples, for those whose entire social existence is an extension of family life', he wrote in *Understanding Media: The Extensions of Man*, 'radio will continue to be a violent experience.'

Shortly after taking over the mailrun, in the summer of 1981, I became radio critic for *Hot Press* magazine. Because I spent most of my day in the van, the radio-cassette player allowed me to inhabit two worlds at once.

In the mornings I listened to RTE Radio One: to the music programme, *Morning Call*, to the eight o'clock news and *It Says in the Papers*, which were repeated at nine, to *The Mike Murphy Show*, *The Gay Byrne Show* and to John Bowman's current affairs programme, *Day by Day*, at eleven o'clock. In the afternoons and evenings I listened to the pop music on Radio Two. When I was on my own in the van, I played the radio loudly, but if there were passengers I would turn the volume down to a dull background murmur.

Strictly speaking, I was not supposed to carry passengers. My father had had a hackney licence for over fifty years, but it could not be handed down with the run. Such licences were the subject of considerable competition, and there was a reputedly rigorous testing of applicants. Since the number of passengers on the route had diminished considerably, and because at the back of my mind I did not really feel that I was going to make a career out of the mailcar, I had never taken the test. This meant that I was not entitled to request fares off any of the passengers, but since my father had always operated an ad hoc system of fare-paying – simply accepting from each individual whatever they offered – in effect nothing had changed. If people offered me money in return for a lift, I was quite at liberty to accept it as a 'gift'. If they did not come forward, no more or less than my father before me, I would never ask.

In truth, the passenger traffic on the runs had fallen off to the extent that such as remained were often more trouble than it was worth purely in financial terms. On a wet and wintry Friday afternoon, it was a far more attractive prospect to be sitting at home by the fire drinking a mug of tea, than to be hunched at the wheel outside Mulligan's in Ballaghaderreen waiting for a few stragglers to finish their shopping. But my father insisted and, as so often in such matters, he was right. It became clear to me that he had never carried these people for the money at all, but because he knew that, without him, many of them would have been left stranded or dependent on the charity of friends or neighbours to take them into town.

The public transport service on this road had never been great: it comprised solely the Galway/Sligo bus which travelled the road mid-morning and teatime. Those who got the bus into Ballaghaderreen would have had to wait all day to get home. Most of them came back in the mailcar. I do not know if this was the crucial factor or not, but sometime in the year or two before I took over the run, some bureaucrat in an office in Dublin or Galway had looked at a map and decided that the bus would be more economic if it went via Lisacul, thereby entirely bypassing the part of the route where my father's best customers lived. My father said that, as long as he was in a position to do anything about it, these people would not be deprived of a way into town; and so I became an unlicensed stagecoach driver.

My father had never had a radio in his van, either in the Thames 800 or in the Transits which he had reluctantly taken to driving when the Thames finally gave up the ghost. We had never had a radio in the house either, though I was never able to establish why. It did not appear to be for the same reason as he mistrusted television, which he had no reservation about denouncing at any and every opportunity. Television he equated with 'pleasure' and 'entertainment', which he identified as the antitheses of work. But this did not appear to be the nature of his objection to radio. In fact, he had a number of crystal sets among his roomfuls of possessions, all of which I presumed must have worked at some time in the past. By the time I stumbled across McLuhan's ideas about radio – that it had 'power to turn the psyche and society into a single echo chamber', that it was 'charged with the resonating echoes of tribal horns and antique drums' – my father was dead.

But even if he had had a radio in the van, my father would rarely, if ever, have listened to it. From reading the *Irish Independent* each day, he was aware of what went on in the world. But to him these were just events, raw and abstract, which came alive only when they became the subject of discussion and argument.

From each of his passengers, from the most vocal to the most withdrawn, he teased opinions and declarations, attitudes and analyses. And if such exchanges ever had the effect of altering his own perspective, the change was never so distinct as to be detectable.

From an early age I was aware that he had some innate capacity to allow people to be themselves in his presence. It was something about his sense of humour, I have always thought, an odd nuance in his laugh, which signalled to almost anyone he met the existence of a common outlook or shared experience.

There was an old man called Harry Raftery who lived alone in a county council cottage about halfway between Loughglynn and Ballaghaderreen. As far as I could tell, he had no family, except a sister who occasionally came to visit, and for most of the time he sat alone in the house, with the door open, gazing out at the road. His face was red and craggy, and you could not look at it without thinking that if you had the time you could read his life story off its lines. It would be a story of hardship and sorrow, of loneliness and disappointment. To most people, Harry spoke in clichés, of which he had two – one benign, the other dark and threatening. If he was in good humour and was not displeased by your presence or demeanour, he would repeat the word 'regimental' over and over again.

'Howya Harry?'

'Regimental.'

'That's a fine day now.'

'Regimental.'

If you displeased him in any way, for instance by interrupting him while he was drinking his bottle of stout in Mulligan's, he would stare into the distance and declaim, 'Don't lose your excitement.' Whenever a neighbour of whom he did not approve got into the van, he would utter this phrase again and again, as though to cow them with its withering rhythm. 'Don't lose your excitement. Don't lose your excitement. Don't lose your excitement.'

Very few people could get much sense out of Harry, but my father was one who could. Harry was a special customer. His age and forbidding mien entitled him to take the front passenger seat, regardless of who else might be in the van. During my father's time at the wheel, when we would stop outside Harry's house on a Thursday, I would immediately jump out and help him up into the front seat.

If someone who did not know the correct protocol was occupying his seat, Harry would climb reluctantly into the back and recite his mantra of displeasure all the way to Ballaghaderreen. But as soon as he was sitting beside my father, the caricature that enclosed him would dissolve. They had an odd ritual for getting into conversation and followed it precisely each day. Harry was a bad sleeper and was almost always awake when my father's van passed his house at about 6.30 on the morning run to Ballaghaderreen. His opening gambit would always be a reference to this.

'It's a long time since you went down this morning, Tom.'

'It is, Harry. It's a long time.' My father would never allow the fear of repetition to interfere with the ritual.

Then Harry would turn around to address the rest of the passengers: 'It's a long time since Tom Waters went down this morning. I was up. I hear him every morning.' With these remarks he drew a line between the front and back sections of the van. Then he and my father would talk – about the weather, about politics, about Harry's sister and her family, about the stretch in the evenings. For perhaps the only time that week, Harry would come alive, would become the person he really was. He would talk up the road to Ballaghaderreen, perched on his seat, pleased as Punch to be the special passenger in the front of Tom Waters's mailcar. He would express his views on the state of the world, on politics and politicians, on whatever his fancy chose. Only occasionally would there be the slightest hint of discord. Harry was a kneejerk Fianna Fáiler, a true believer, and sometimes, for pure devilment, my father would tease him about 'Babyface' Lynch, or say the proverbial 'bad word' about de Valera, whereupon Harry would temporarily descend to his mantra-chanting self: 'Don't lose your excitement. Don't lose your excitement.' Such occasions, however, were rare.

By the time I took over the run full-time, Harry had become a much less frequent traveller. His health had declined: he had fallen victim to arthritis and now moved out only with great difficulty. But now and again I would see the shopping bag placed on the grass margin outside Harry's house and would pull in and help him aboard the van. We made an odd couple in the front: me, long-haired and leather-jacketed; he, crippled and becapped. To look at us, you could not help thinking that we must have had precious little in common, but he saw beyond my long hair and leather jacket to the single fact which was of significance to him: that I was Tom Waters's son. This allowed us to communicate across a gap which would otherwise have been unbridgeable.

'It's a long time since you went down this morning, John,' he would say, as soon as he was settled. Then he would talk to me in the same way as he had talked to my father, earnestly and intimately, as though we were as one before the world.

It was with Harry that I first noticed the effect of the radio. He had no television in his house, but he had a wireless, the dial of which, as with many such sets in the country, was permanently fixed at Athlone, the only control operated over the set being by way of the on/off switch. Harry's set was more off than on. He turned it on in the morning for the News, but switched off again almost immediately afterwards. I found this strange, since I would have imagined that the radio would be company for him. Whenever the subject came up, perhaps in relation to some item on *The Gay Byrne Show*, he would explain that he always switched off after the News to save the batteries, but I suspect that there was more to it than this. The effect on him of the van's radio went some way towards solving the puzzle. If I had the radio turned up, perhaps to follow a running political story, he would lapse into silence and then, having listened for a few minutes, pronounce, 'There's a fierce lot of smart men above there in Dublin.'

I was aware that the reason Harry did not listen to the radio was that he did not know what to make of much of what it poured forth. It was not that he did not understand what was being said, nor that this was, in the conventional sense, 'over his head', but that the tone and content in no way related to his life or to his view of the world. The talk was about places he had never been and did not recognise; it was like radio from another country. If I did not take my cue to turn down the radio, he would immediately lapse into his customary ejaculations: 'Don't lose your excitement. Don't lose your excitement.'

Harry's was an extreme case of alienation from the radio, but often in such extremes we get to see the truth. Throughout the early years of the 1980s, I was to see the same thing recur, to only slightly varying extents, again and again. Since I was writing a radio review column, I had often, with an impending deadline, to leave the radio turned up, even if this displeased my passengers. And usually it did displease them. The early eighties are remembered in the conventional wisdom of the Irish communications media as a time 'of great change' in Irish life. Political scandal followed scandal, as election after election failed to deliver a decisive result. The abortion amendment debate raged across the public airwaves. Private tragedies, like the death of Ann Lovett and her baby in a grotto in Granard, seeped on to the public agenda. People went on *Day by Day* and *The Gay Byrne Show* to air their views about modern Ireland. They identified themselves as 'liberals', 'progressives', sometimes even as 'radicals'. They spoke about 'Irishness' a great deal, and about the meaning this had for them.

Each discussion began with a specific theme – abortion, divorce, contraception – but the underlying agenda related to something more profound and fundamental: what kind of people we were, what we wanted to become, and who was standing in the way of progress and change. At some time, not long before, an invisible line had been drawn across the path between The Past and Modern Ireland. It was as though a count of heads was being undertaken to establish how many people were on either side of the line. Mobility between the two appeared almost unthinkable. The two Irelands had value systems that had little or no common ground. Those who lived in the past were taken to give their allegiance to the Catholic Church, the land and Fianna Fáil – loyalties that then became synonymous in the mouths of their Modern Ireland accusers. These, in turn, outrightly rejected this model of Irishness – we were an urban people, they insisted, a modern industrialised state with an emerging class system. They spoke disparagingly about de Valera's dancing-at-the-crossroads vision of a people content with hard work and simple pleasures. We needed urgently to rescue our political structures from the grip of the tribal politics of Fianna Fáil.

Those speaking for Modern Ireland appeared to regard whole sections of the country as priest-ridden, tribal and untouchable. An attachment to the land, they averred, was no longer a defining feature of what it was to be Irish; on the contrary, it appeared to disqualify large sections of the population from membership of *their* Ireland. Their vision seemed to have been fashioned entirely as the antithesis of the past. If de Valera said black, then the correct position must be white. Certain issues were always close to the surface, but were never touched upon – issues like God, faith and the natural world. These became unmentionables. To refer by name to one or other of these concepts was immediately to be branded a 'conservative'. Everything was reduced to the dry, neutral language of ideology and conceptual politics. There seemed to be an unspoken suggestion that those who wished to belong to their Modern Ireland would have to leave behind all the nonsense of the past.

To listen to the radio, one would think that the entire country was tearing itself apart. And yet, if you looked around the landscape of this selfsame country, there was no visible sign of dissonance. Most of the people seemed to be going about their business pretty much as normal. Unlike many of the people who travelled with me, I could connect with the Ireland from which these programmes were broadcast. It was an Ireland impatient with reality, and in some ways I belonged to it more than I belonged where I was.

This put me more or less on the opposite side to many of the people I ferried in and out of town. But it was impossible not to be aware of the feeling of alienation that many such people were beginning to feel as a result of the continuous verbal assault from the capital. In the early stages, they found some amusement in the passionate hostility of their accusers. Yet, as the debate wore on, they became indifferent to it, but with a guarded, defensive indifference. Then they switched off, or drowned out the talk on the radio with their own, more pressing concerns.

None of the issues being discussed were new to the passengers in the van. Many of them had lived long lives, had travelled half across the globe, to America, where they had earned a living for themselves and for their families back home. There was nothing in the talk on the radio that was outside their experience of the world. And yet there was something about the way it was being debated, something about the tone of the discussion, which turned them off, tuned them out. They did not recognise themselves in the radio's descriptions of a priest-ridden, backward and reactionary people. Most or all of them were Catholics, yes, but the nature of their Catholicism could not be taken for granted in the manner their accusers appeared to believe. Their faith was as complex and individual as the pattern of lines on their faces.

When they talked among themselves, their opinions clearly derived not from the tablets handed down by their pastors, but from within, from their innermost personalities and experience. They knew about the realities of life, and they did not have a naive or ostrich-like attitude to issues like abortion or divorce. The things that so preoccupied the radio in those days were also the currency of their own social intercourse. They would talk quietly about such and such a girl from the far side of the lake who had 'got into trouble'. From time to time there would be muted mention of such a girl having gone 'across the water'. The range of response would be at least as wide as any radio programme might offer on the political issue of abortion, but there would be a far greater leavening of humanity, of tolerance, of compassion.

And, yet, the Great Abortion Debate of 1983 had little or no meaning for such people. Perhaps this was to some extent because the word 'abortion' was not one they themselves would use, any more than they would use the word 'cancer'. Cancer was referred to as 'The Buck'. Abortion was not given a name. But there was more to it than this. Something had happened to drive a wedge between these people and the society in which they lived. It was as though they sensed that such debate was not to be taken at face value, as though the issue was not the subject under discussion, but something far deeper, something that excluded them.

I did not know what side I was supposed to be on in this battle for the soul of the Irish nation. I did not feel in the least bit priest-ridden, and had long since stopped going to mass. I was in favour of divorce, and had never voted for Fianna Fáil in my life. I had even written articles in *Hot Press* making fun of Sean Doherty. Like most of my friends around town, I had an arm's-length relationship with the Catholic Church. I had suffered the brunt of its violence, from the nuns and brothers who had taught me as a child, but I had long since decided to go my own way, a choice that I was in no way penalised for making. I remained on good terms with several of the priests in Castlerea. In many ways the Church, for all the talk of its oppressiveness, remained a benign force in that society, as in the instance of the Canon's intervention on my father's behalf. People like my father were genuinely mystified when the Church was discussed as an institution, rather than the body of individuals, good and bad, which he recognised.

And so, although I approved of most of what the voices on the radio wanted to achieve, I did not like their tone, which was hectoring and dismissive, as though they wished to punish rather than persuade, as though the issue – of abortion, contraception, clientelism or corruption – was not something to be talked about in isolation but was part of one big problem, a problem that was, by implication, the fault of some vague, never-quite-delineated section of the Irish people.

This mood achieved its apotheosis in the early months of 1984, following the deaths of fifteen-year-old Ann Lovett and her newborn infant boy in the grotto of Granard churchyard. It was just a few months since the Irish electorate had passed an amendment to the Constitution – asserting the right to life of the unborn child – and the two events immediately became connected in the public imagination. The Dublin media descended on Granard, and, as though to exact revenge for the defeat of the liberal opposition to the amendment, pointed their collective finger at the nature of the society in which Ann Lovett had lived. Here, they said, were the fruits of the reactionary forces that had advocated the amendment, an example of the oppressive and hypocritical nature of the priest-ridden rural Ireland which had given support to the constitutional amendment. The voices on the radio increased in number and volume.

There seemed to be loose in the land a new form of tyranny, at least as unpleasant as that which these voices told us they wished to remove. In its unrelenting onslaught, I observed a part of the Irish public shrivel itself up into a foetal hunch and stare fixedly out of the window of my green Hiace van.

8

Smoke Along the Track

I did not write about this dissonance in my *Hot Press* radio column or in any of my other articles for the magazine at that time. Because I was starting out in journalism, I wrote the kind of articles that I believed would be most likely to get published. I rapidly became adept at doing this.

But looking back at many of those articles now, I detect a dissonance in them which ingrained itself without my noticing. They contain many of the stock images of rural Ireland that I now recognise as originating in the Dublin – and in particular the Dublin media's – view of the country. Most of the articles were about rock music, the culture of which, in Castlerea, was no different than elsewhere. It was a neutral force within the society where I lived, having meaning only for particular members of particular generations.

Rock had been almost exclusively the terrain of the townies, and, since most of them had left to work in Dublin, London or America, country and western was again the dominant musical form. For most people, rock was an alien presence, to be regarded sceptically and ironically, though in the main with tolerance. To continue to be a rock fan was to make some kind of statement about yourself, but mainly it was a statement you made *to* yourself.

As indeed, as far as Castlerea was concerned, were the articles I wrote for *Hot Press*. Only one shop, Mulvihill's, stocked the magazine. I asked Mrs Mulvihill one day how many copies of *Hot Press* she sold. Three, she said. Since I myself bought two, one of which I lent around to friends, this left only one other person in the entire town who was aware of my fame as a rock journalist. One morning I was leaving Mulvihill's, having just bought the morning paper, when I heard a voice behind me asking Mrs Mulvihill for the latest *Hot Press*. I turned around to see a fellow townie from Church Road, whom I knew only remotely, rolling up the magazine and putting it in his pocket. At least, I reflected, there is one other person in this kip of a town who is aware of my contribution to the literature of popular culture. In order to bask a little in the gaze of my newfound following, I loitered momentarily in the doorway to allow him to pass me by. 'Hello, Tommy,' he said as he squeezed past.

Perhaps he did not recognise me in the articles I wrote. They painted an odd picture of the landscape we both inhabited. One such article will serve as an example. It was a review of a concert by Matt Molloy, the Ballaghaderreen-born flute-player, and Mick Hanly, the Limerick singer and songwriter, who had played formerly with the rock band Moving Hearts. The concert took place in the Tulsk Inn, a big barn of a public house in the eponymous village on the main road between Strokestown and Ballinagare. When I arrived in the pub, the first person I saw was a priest. He was drunk. In my article I called him Father GUBU. He was not from Tulsk, but was passing through on his way from the races in Roscommon.

'You have lovely big breasts', I quoted him as saying to a female fellow-customer, in my review of the gig in the *Hot Press* of 4 May 1984. 'I'd like to put my head in between them.'

'Ah sure, it's perishin' weather altogether, Father.'

'I'd like to take you home with me,' he elaborated, his hand hovering around the woman's knee.

'It's very cold, right enough, Father,' the woman replied loudly. 'For the time of year.'

At this point, my article noted, the musicians came on.

With one, so to speak, almighty bound, the Reverend GUBU was out on the middle of the floor, his thoughts on a different kind of flute.

'Mattie Molloy! Mattie Molloy! Mattie Molloy from Ballaghaderreen!'

Waving a rosary beads and spouting Latin to beat the band, the unprecedented priest approached our table and proceeded to impart his blessing on the assembled imbibers, two ashtrays, twenty Major and several pints of Smithwicks draught.

'*Benedicat vos omnipotens Deus, Pater et filius et spiritus sanctus.*'

'Amen, I mean ahem. But sure, so long as the rain keeps off, eh?'

Everything in this article occurred as I said it did. The 'facts', as a journalist would have it, were correct. And yet, in a different sense, there was not an ounce of truth in it.

Just because something 'happens', because it is 'true', because the 'facts' are correct, does not ensure that it is the truth. Truth is in the eye of the reader. The readers of *Hot Press* were, in the main, like the people who wrote for *Hot Press*. They had a particular view of Ireland: they believed, for example, that it was a regressive, oppressed and priest-ridden country. My article served to bear out a prejudice on their part that the priests, whom they perceived as attempting to dictate to them how to conduct their private lives, were drunks and sex maniacs all. Since this is what they believed, this is what they liked to read in *Hot Press*. By writing it, I was reinforcing their prejudice. The priest in Tulsk was every bit as drunk and as lecherous as I said he was, but not only was he an exception, but his behaviour that night was quite exceptional even (as I discovered afterwards) for himself. The woman he had tried to grope understood this, and so did I.

It is a strange thing to go back to things you wrote several years ago and realise that the part of you that wrote them has died. When I wrote an article on something about which I could not make up my mind, or was ambiguous about, I split myself in two and attributed the views I had doubts about to someone called 'Cryptic Jim'. I do not have a clear picture in my head of what Cryptic Jim looked like, but I know that he was about the same age as myself, and from a similar background. He was an amateur sociologist.

Once, for example, I wrote an article about Big Tom, the country and western singer. I had ambiguous feelings about Big Tom. Big Tom was for culchies. We in the town were into more refined outfits, like Horslips and The Freshmen. We were living in the Universal City. We were a race apart from the culchies, who came to town dressed in sports coats and with their shirt collars open wide across their shoulders. We dressed for the part we had fantasised for ourselves: we wore platform shoes, denim jeans, and scoop-neck T-shirts, bought from the mail order adverts at the back of the *New Musical Express*. We poured scorn on country and western. All the same, we always went to Big Tom's dances, because he brought in the women from miles around the town, and from towns miles away, far-flung places like Ballyhaunis and Ballyfarnon.

Townies rarely danced at Big Tom's dances. We always pretended that this was because the music he played, an odd hybrid which had the name of 'country and Irish', was too simple-minded for us. But the truth was that few of us had ever learned to jive. To us townies, the jive was a dance of extraordinary complexity and precision. It began with the male taking his partner's hands in his and swinging her backwards and forwards until they had gathered sufficient momentum to let go one of her hands and allow her to spin round while still holding on to the other. The couple would then perform several variations on this – first the man would do it with his right hand, then with his left, then he would let go of the woman entirely, giving her a spin as he did so, and catching her two hands in his as she returned to face him.

Much of the action and activity of the dance was performed by the female, but she remained at all times within her partner's control. The jive enabled the male to participate fully in a dance of apparently great intricacy while managing to appear totally disinterested in what he was doing. It allowed country men, who felt uncomfortable in their Sunday suits, to communicate with women without speaking and without losing their sense of composure. Romances grew from a couple's ability to jive together, as frequently as they did out of compatibility in other matters. The more permanent the relationship, the more complex and dexterous became their embellishment of the jive. We townies watched the culchies with extravagant disdain as they swung each other around the dance-floor, but secretly longed to be able to perform this mysterious manoeuvre. The jive gave the culchies one of their few opportunities for rubbing our noses in it. They danced their heads off while we stood at the edge of the dance-floor, pretending to be totally bored with the proceedings.

There was an intoxicating quality to Big Tom, something comforting about the crush of a Big Tom crowd, and about the sentiments in his lyrics. This was how you felt, in spite of yourself: 'I'll always be a drifter/But I'll be driftin' back/To where I left you cryin'/In the smoke along the track.' And there was something funny about him, which had not been adequately comprehended in the mundane and superior-minded jokes we would make about him and his followers. Since I had begun writing for *Hot Press*, it had been my ambition to write an article about Big Tom which would hint at what he had come to mean in the place I came from. In November 1983 he appeared on the cover of *Hot Press*. This is how I described him:

On stage, Big Tom, dressed in a red jacket, white pants and a white, open-necked shirt, is surrounded by half-a-dozen men, half his age, wearing black pants, red shirts and bright sequined waistcoats. Big Tom, singing Country, alternates at the mike with a man with tight pants and an indoor hairdo who sings the 'pops' and does all the introductions. Big Tom rarely speaks, if at all. The 'pops' are awful, but some of the country songs are incredible, mixing melancholia with an unerring comic vision. Big Tom is all business. He hardly ever moves his big frame, except to walk up to, and away from, the microphone. He's cheerful, winking in his odd slow way at the odd punter, mostly the women. But overall, he has the look of a man who would be much happier behind the wheel of a muckspreader than a guitar.

Notice the final, cop-out line? The rest of the article was the same: evasions, false ironies, falsehoods. Cryptic Jim earned his money that week:

He was in the right place at the right time. He stepped into the vacuum created by the commandeering of rural Ireland's indigenous folk music by the prim-faced, fáinne-wearing, sensible-shoed culture vultures. He put his finger on the pulse and provided a surrogate folk music. He gave the people what they wanted: songs about their own joys and sorrows, their exiles and reunions, their lovers and their mothers. Plus, Big Tom looked perfect. He wasn't a star symbol, but the opposite. Like John Wayne, he looked ordinary, only indestructibly so. You will observe that Big Tom's face resembles the side of a mountain. It is cracked and weatherbeaten, and it doesn't so much grow old as erode. He is therefore the obvious symbol of the Old standing against the New invading culture. If you happened to be reading the *Irish Times* of September 9th last, you may have noticed a map detailing the pattern of the voting in the so-called abortion referendum. And you may also have noted that Glenamaddy – which, as we know, is the centre of the kingdom in which Big Tom's rule is still absolute – was slap-bang in the middle of the area which returned the biggest Yes vote in the country. Now, this is neither coincidence, nor, as some prejudiced interests have suggested, conclusive evidence of a massive reactionary culture counterwave sweeping in from the west coast.

In my view [Jim concluded] the Amendment result in rural Ireland represents not so much an active hostile opposition to what are called the New, Urban, Liberal, Intellectual values, as merely a passive indifference to them. Similarly with Big Tom: the closing-in of his audience around him is symptomatic, not so much of hostility towards what we might call the New Polycultural Salad, peddled by the mass media, as a sort of disinterested passivity towards it. The underlying cause of both of these phenomena is much closer to lethargy than it is to reaction.

I could not have put it better myself.

9

The Parable of the Fat Chieftain

During the seventies, when Charlie Haughey and his friend P. J. Mara drove around Ireland on what was known as the chicken and chips circuit, it is likely that they regularly crisscrossed my father's mailcar run. This is what democracy does to politicians: drags them down to earth, makes it harder for them to lose the run of themselves. For how can someone who has had to endure such indignity to get elected ever lose sight of the source of his power?

The two vehicles might never have met, but their occupants were of one mind. They all had decided that the destiny of their country depended on the accession to power of Charles J. Haughey.

Haughey's belief in this inevitability was perhaps understandably transparent, though far more complex than is commonly understood. My father's was part idealism and part perversity. He really did believe that Haughey offered the best chance the country had, but was altogether more attracted by the fact that almost all the people he least identified with in Irish public life – people like Conor Cruise O'Brien and Garret FitzGerald – had decided that Haughey would return more or less over their dead bodies. The positive aspects of his faith in Haughey's reascent to high office, therefore, were inextricably bound up with anticipatory glee at what consternation such an eventuality would bring down on the people whose dislike for Haughey was perhaps matched only by my father's suspicion of them.

Haughey chewed chicken and chips by night, and my father proselytised on his behalf by day. He never called him 'Charles Haughey', or 'C.J.', but simply 'Haughey' or 'Charlie', depending on the demeanour of the person he was talking to at the time.

From time to time, someone would attempt to stir the sediment of latent passions, as the argument swung back and forth over the ropes in the Thames 800.

'Sure, what has that fellow in common with the likes of us, and he with a big mansion above there in Dublin? Not to mention boats and helicopters to beat the band?'

'Arrah, what about it? Sure if he made himself rich, mightn't he make us rich as well?'

My father would let the argument rage on, sometimes pulling his handkerchief out to wipe the tears of laughter from his eyes. I had never known a subject to entertain him so much. In the end, he would invariably make the same declaration: 'In parts of Africa, where people don't have half enough to eat, people always like to have a fat chief. They think: if he is well-fed, at least he is a man who knows how to feed himself. And if he can feed himself, sure mightn't he be able to feed a few more of us as well. So the first thing you do if you want to be chief is fatten yourself up.

'Of course,' he would add after a pause, 'there'll always

be someone to say that if he's as fat as he is, then it must be because he left some other poor devil with only half enough to eat.'

As I grew into my twenties, in the same way as I communicated with my friends through talking about rock music, politics became perhaps the only language of proper communication between myself and my father. By 'politics', I mean politics as we had been born to them. My own 'politics' were different: I considered myself a sort of socialist, though I knew little about the theory of Marxism and as little as most other Irish socialists about the reality of its practice.

My 'socialism' was as much a reaction to what I perceived to be the betrayed promise of my generation, to the lack of opportunity in my life and surroundings, as my father's championing of Haughey was a reaction to the attitude of the chanters of the 'flawed pedigree' smear.

But politics, as talked about in the van, in the pubs, or in the streets of the town, was a different animal to the politics we heard discussed on the radio. The measure of a politician was his ability to get things done on behalf of not just his supporters but his constituents in general. A politician was a fixer of last resort: when you did not know what else to do about a problem, you consulted your TD. For some people, the line of last resort occurred at a much earlier stage than for others, but it was not the politician's function, nor in his interest, to comment on this. The sure sign of a successful politician was to hear someone say that, even though they had never voted for him, he had delivered some assistance that had not been obtained from other sources. If someone had already tried his own party's TD, without success, and had gone over to the other side and been helped, there was a very high likelihood that the vote, too, would change sides in the next election. Throughout the early years of the 1980s, I heard this comment made about one politician with far more frequency than about any other local politician. That politician was Sean Doherty.

If you listened to the radio, of course, you would know that such activity was frowned upon. It was known as 'clientelism', and if you paid careful attention, you realised that even the politicians who most objected to it had become very adept at its practice. They resented having to do it, and they resented those who were better at it than they were.

Cryptic Jim understood clientelism, and approved of it thoroughly, but I myself, being a 'socialist', did not. I agreed with the voices on the radio. It seemed natural, therefore, that I should be opposed to everything for which Sean Doherty stood.

When there was trouble with the mailrun – the van needed a new engine and we could not afford it – my father and I would discuss the problem in calm and measured terms, and then would have a fight about Sean Doherty. My father liked and admired Doherty; he believed he was a decent man and a good politician. The fact that he was also on the Haughey wing of Fianna Fáil, and a loyal spear-carrier, was icing on the cake. But he never defended Doherty as passionately as when others – and particularly outsiders – were attacking him.

Throughout the period of the 1982–87 coalition, Doherty would be the subject of much discussion, though little debate. In a large part of the public imagination, he had come to personify all those characteristics in a politician which were to be avoided at all costs. His name had become shorthand for a particular political condition: he was the archetypal rural redneck who had been corrupted by a couple of whiffs of real power. Words seemed to cling to him and then to swell up into malign tumours of suggested improbity, menace and political malodorousness. Dowra, for example, was the name of a small village in County Cavan in which, one morning in September 1982, a man was due to appear in court as a witness in an assault case in which the defendant was Sean Doherty's brother-in-law. But on the morning of the court case, the witness was arrested by the RUC at the home of a friend across the border and so was prevented from giving evidence. Doherty's intervention was suspected, though never proved.

Dowra came to be imagined in the public mind as a place of perpetual darkness, a place where strange and improbable things occurred. Even for people who did not know where the village was, or precisely what significance it possessed in the Doherty legend, the word 'Dowra' somehow came to encapsulate all the sins that were to be laid at Sean Doherty's door: how he had tapped the telephones of two leading political journalists, Bruce Arnold of the *Irish Independent* and Geraldine Kennedy of the *Sunday Tribune*, because he believed them to be involved in a conspiracy with anti-Haughey members of Fianna Fáil to remove Haughey as leader of the party, and therefore also as Taoiseach; how he had assisted a fellow minister, Ray MacSharry, in bugging a conversation between MacSharry and one of the anti-Haughey wing, Martin O'Donoghue, in which MacSharry suspected that he might be offered a bribe to withdraw his support from

Haughey. 'Bugging': there was another word, a word for people to roll around on their tongues, a word that seemed to embody all the sinister undercurrents which swirled around the depths of the GUBU year of 1982.

My father did not adopt either the conventional Fine Gael view of Doherty as demon, or the Fianna Fáil orthodoxy that all his misfortunes were the result of a conspiracy by the enemies of Haughey. He simply looked at the line-up on either side, and aligned himself with Doherty. Although he had been a supporter of Haughey's leadership of Fianna Fáil, he had not so far deviated from his lifelong election-day pattern of giving his first preference to Fine Gael. Now this too was about to change. When the same people who despised Haughey told us that Doherty's behaviour over the phone-tapping and the bugging of a ministerial conversation was a disgrace to the country and its politics, my father began to talk openly of voting Fianna Fáil.

My own received loathing for Doherty occasionally spilled over into print. Once, in the middle of my *Hot Press* radio column, I mentioned that I came from 'the constituency which, to my eternal shame, elected Sean Doherty'. The following week, a ministerial Mercedes pulled up in the road outside Frenchpark post office, allowing its occupants to stare at me sitting in the Hiace van. This was the thing about Doherty: he seemed to know almost everything, and even when he didn't, he had a way of making you think that maybe he knew more than you imagined.

For those of us who, willingly or otherwise, qualified as his constituents in those early years of the eighties, Doherty defined the thoughts we had, not just about him, but about our relationship to the place in which we lived.

It became impossible to be indifferent to him; you had to be either with him or against him. If you were against him, it became harder to live in a place where such intense loyalty to him existed, not because of anything he or his followers might say or do, but because of the way you yourself interpreted the meaning of his popularity. What did it say about Roscommon? What did it say about your ability to continue to live there? What kind of statement did your continuing to live there make about you?

Those years passed like a blur. First he rose, then he fell. And the further and harder he fell in the estimation of the voices on the radio, the more his reputation soared in Roscommon.

The Fine Gael/Labour coalition, returned to office in November 1982, released details of Doherty's phone-tapping activities during his brief tenure as Minister for Justice. *Today Tonight* came to Boyle and conducted an investigation of his wrongdoing, exposing the way he had attempted to interfere with the local *gardaí* in the pursuit of their duty. There were rumours that he knew far more about everything that had happened than he was prepared to say. It was said in the constituency that he had photocopied every document in the Department of Justice before leaving. He gave an interview to *Magill* magazine in which he spoke enigmatically about documents and transcripts: 'I wonder would we ever find those transcripts.' These were transcripts of telephone conversations that allegedly had been acquired on his behalf. Their discovery, he said, would vindicate him. 'I know how we'd find them. We'd look at all the stones until we found one with no moss, and then we'd look under it.'

His supporters cheered and mobbed him wherever he

went. For a time there were functions and processions in his honour in what seemed like every barn and at every crossroads in the constituency. I sneaked in the door of one such function in the Casino Ballroom in Castlerea, and scanned the hundreds of dancing couples for Sean Doherty's mocking smile. At last I saw him, spinning a woman around with one hand, as though she were a top. I watched him dance for a while before leaving.

He was the best jiver I had ever seen.

10

Darkness on the Edge of Town

The first day of May 1984 was a beautiful sunny morning, the likes of which I had been looking forward to for much of the previous eight months. I drove to Dublin from Castlerea, hardly taking in the glorious weather. My heart was heavy and yet its weight had a momentum of its own: like a hearse in top gear. I was on my way to Dublin to start work full-time with *Hot Press*, having left the mailcar behind.

It was the hardest thing I had ever had to do. I felt as if I had swum out to rescue a drowning man, but he had begun to struggle and so I had, there and then, to make an entirely rational decision to save myself or allow the two of us to drown. I swam and swam and tried not to look behind.

All things considered, my father had taken it well. The run was becoming increasingly uneconomic. I knew a bit about engines but nothing near as much as my father did, and as the Hiace became older and more decrepit, the repair bills mounted. Moreover, there was growing talk in the post office that, now that it was being run by a semi-state company, An Post, serious cutbacks were in the offing. These were expected to include most of the sub-offices to which my father had delivered the mail for the previous fifty years. When I told him I had been offered a job in Dublin, he said that I must do what I thought best. The run meant everything to him, but he could not guarantee that it would be there after he was gone. I might never again get the chance I was now getting.

I had had serious reservations about leaving my parents in a far from financially secure situation, but by a stroke of luck I had stumbled upon a minor goldmine amongst the account books that my father had kept of his transactions with the Department of Posts and Telegraphs and his newspaper clients. I noticed that several of the routes we had been serving did not appear to be covered by any of the regular cheque payments. When I asked him about it, my father said that the runs in question were 'in dispute' – he had been attempting to negotiate a proper rate for them, but had had difficulty in bringing the newspaper companies to the bargaining table.

Despite this, so as not to disoblige the newsagents on the routes, my father had continued to deliver the newspapers every morning. I asked him how long this had been going on. Thirteen years, he told me. After a brief bout of intense negotiation with the three main newspaper companies, I managed to arrive at a satisfactory arrangement whereby my father effectively could retire without any immediate financial worries. I could depart with a more restful mind, if not a lighter heart.

Those of us who leave what we call 'the country' for what is described as 'the city' are conditioned to believe that we have entered a different culture. This is not so. It is true that we become temporarily overawed by the size of the city, but this is mere confusion, not culture-shock. The difference between a city like Dublin and a town like Castlerea is a difference of scale, not sensibility.

This is just one of the many ways in which we choose to divide ourselves, to create modern tribes to satisfy our atavistic craving for taking sides. For such a small country, we are awfully good at dividing ourselves up. 'Northern' Ireland and 'Southern' Ireland, 'Urban' Ireland and 'Rural' Ireland, the 'Old' and the 'New' Irelands. Throughout history, we seem to have made a habit of dividing ourselves and being conquered by others.

Within Irish society today, there are perhaps three smaller 'Irelands' – three subsections – two of which are clear-cut and discernibly obvious, and one that is nothing of the kind. 'Rural' Ireland and 'Urban' Ireland, at first sight at least, appear to be self-evident entities, the respective territories of what in the simple good old days were know as Culchie and Jackeen. When I was growing up, this was the great rivalry. Dublin was identified with people with hard, Joxer accents who made fun of people from the country. The two sides met on very rare occasions, like the All-Ireland Final, when they would throw harmless abuse at each other outside Croke Park, occasionally resorting to fisticuffs.

At some point in the late seventies or early eighties, when we in the West of Ireland became conscious for the first time that the voices on the radio and the television were not our voices, we automatically began to think of them as Dublin voices. But the odd thing about them is that in many instances they were indeed our voices, speaking with accents very much like our own. Certainly they were not the accents we associated with Dublin. What we really felt was that they were not saying things with which we could sympathise, and they certainly did not seem to sympathise with us.

They lambasted us for our conservatism, for our backward notions of politics, for our profligacy with public money. Whenever something was suggested which might be of benefit to what they called 'rural Ireland' or 'the country', they seemed to be against it. When it snowed in Dublin, the airwaves came alive with talk about snow; when it snowed in 'the country', they spoke disparagingly about 'the country coming to a standstill after a couple of showers of sleet'. Since they spoke from Dublin, and seemed to dislike 'the country' so much, we thought they just had to be Dubliners.

It was not long before it occurred to me that there were at least two Dublins. At first I did not know how to define them to myself, but to some crude extent they appeared to be geographically divided by the river Liffey. When you crossed over O'Connell Bridge from the southside, you became aware within a few yards that you were among different people than you had been encountering just a couple of streets before. Something about their appearance and dress set them apart. The men wore leather jackets, windcheaters, jumpers, T-shirts, sneakers and white socks. The women all seemed to have their hair dyed blond. They spoke with rough, Joxer accents. These were the Dubliners of the tribal rivalry, the Dubliners who had defined the capital for me in my youth. But they did not belong to the Dublin which had hectored us from the airwaves, any more than did the people of Roscommon. If this was the real Dublin, then these people were outsiders in their own city, confined to a northside reservation, away from the thriving heart of 'official' Dublin.

Less than a mile away, on the southside, on Grafton Street, Baggot Street and Merrion Row, were the people I had heard on the radio. This was 'official' Dublin, a thriving metropolis inhabited by well-heeled and fashionable people who, as they themselves would have it, 'worked hard and played hard'. This Dublin was the centre of the nation's economy, government and media. The other Dublin was the place we had seen from time to time when it was being patronised on *Today Tonight* – a Dublin of poverty, neglect, alienation, drug addiction and very little hope of real change. In this Dublin were the people I had always thought of as Dubliners, but they did not seem to belong in their own city, looking harassed, weatherbeaten and old before their time. When the two Dublins came into contact, it was either by accident or for the purposes of the war that was being waged between them – a war called crime.

For someone coming up from 'the country', there is very little incentive to become part of the 'real' Dublin. It is a much too unpleasant place, squalid and ugly. Its people are without optimism. They have no stake in the city's future, and no future themselves, other than the prospect of life in a working-class ghetto which will be created for them on the fringes of the city when the market dictates that official Dublin is ready to expand on to the ground they instinctively call home. Because they are Dubliners by name, but are not part of official Dublin, they feel unable to call their city their own, and so do not extend the hand of friendship to outsiders.

The newly blown-in culchie has two choices: to retire

to one of the culchie reservations that have grown up on the southside of the city – to a bedsit in Ranelagh or Rathmines – or to attempt to integrate himself into the fiction that is official Dublin. If the former, he will end up in a twilight southside world which mirrors the bleak, forbidding landscape of the northside, where culchies survive in bedsit accommodation all week and go home to the country at the weekend. If the latter, he will have to learn to live in the official Dublin, while turning a blind eye to the reality it denies.

Most of the people I had heard on the radio had opted to take this latter course. They collectively made up what had become known as 'Dublin 4', a phrase that had cropped up with increasing frequency in the years since the ascent to power of the Garret FitzGerald-led coalition of November 1982. It had come to mean something real but nebulous in the language of modern Irish politics.

I soon realised that there was a clear distinction to be made between 'Dublin 4' and Dublin 4, for the appellation applied to two almost totally separate entities: one a geographical location, the other a cast of mind. There was but an increasingly tenuous connection between the two. The term, as properly and originally applied, referred to a postal district of Dublin. These subdivisions were introduced by the post office in the early sixties, to cope with postal deliveries to a capital expanding in all directions. The postal subdivisions radiate outwards from Dublin 1, which embraces the city centre north of the Liffey, to Dublin 24, which includes Tallaght, Jobstown and Rathcoole in the south-west. Odd numbers denoted north, even numbers south. The districts were created for convenience of delivery, and reflected neither economic factors nor natural geographical or community boundaries.

The Dublin 4 postal district embraced the upmarket locations of Ballsbridge, Donnybrook, Merrion and Sandymount, but also the southside working-class communities of Ringsend and Irishtown. The core of the area was the Pembroke district, formerly the estate of Lord Pembroke, which at one time had its own urban district council but was amalgamated into the City of Dublin in 1930. Up to the 1920s, the area was identified primarily with the unionist ascendancy who owned the big houses along the leafy avenues of Shrewsbury and Ailesbury Roads, Clyde Road and the streets around Herbert Park. Their servants lived in cottages on Beatty's Avenue, Ballsbridge Avenue and Estate Cottages.

A major factor in the evolving perception of this part of Dublin 4 as the most affluent in the city was the introduction in the 1940s of the Irish version of the boardgame Monopoly, which equated Shrewsbury Road and Ailesbury Road with, respectively, London's Mayfair and Park Lane. Following the parliamentary election of 1918, in which a Donnybrook man, Desmond FitzGerald, was elected to represent Pembroke at Westminster, he and a small coterie of his fellow Cumann na nGaedheal ministers became known as the 'Donnybrook Set'. This term was resurrected and redeployed in the 1980s by the Mayo-born journalist John Healy, who used it as a stick to beat the coalition government of FitzGerald's son, Garret. Healy had a habit of stealing and storing such terms, magpie-like, for use when an occasion arose. As with many of his creations, he deliberately and wilfully adapted language and reality to the purpose of creating a greater truth; the terms 'Donnybrook Set' and 'Dublin 4' became synonymous Healyisms, referring to the Fine Gael ascendancy of 'Garret the Good' and the 'national handlers' – Healy's phrase for the small bunch of media advisers with whom FitzGerald surrounded himself.

But it was more than just a convenient moniker to channel criticism of an unpopular government: its truth went far beyond that, and was recognised by people from a wide range of backgrounds as crystallising something on the political landscape not in tune with themselves.

There were as many definitions of 'Dublin 4' as there were perceptions of it. Its most general usage, however, was as a pejorative term to describe what was effectively a new class of people, whose principal characteristic was perceived as a stridently professed aversion to unreconstructed forms of Catholicism and nationalism, but in particular to Fianna Fáil, and most especially to Charles J. Haughey.

In one respect the only existence that 'Dublin 4' has is in the perception of those who resent it. For 'Dublin 4' people did not so describe themselves. In the first place, most of them lived outside the Dublin 4 postal district: in Dublin 6, Blackrock, Howth, or Foxrock. Garret FitzGerald himself had lived for many years in Rathmines, and had not had a house in Dublin 4 since the mid-seventies. Though coined to goad him, the phrase, as commonly used in the late eighties, had detached itself from the personality of FitzGerald, who by then had retired to the backbenches, abandoned by the Dublin 4 brigade whose darling he had been for a decade.

If put to the pin of your collar, you might have said that the 'Dublin 4' species had become synonymous with the kind of people who frequented particular pubs and restaurants, most of which, like the Shelbourne Hotel, the Unicorn Restaurant, and Doheny & Nesbitt's public house, were actually within a biscuit's throw of each other in Dublin 2. These were the equivalent of what in London were known as the 'chattering classes': people who, through their jobs in the media, the civil service and the professions, were in a position to influence the direction of society in an intravenous manner, and who were not shy about giving vent to their opinions at every available opportunity.

The actual geographical location of Dublin 4 was blameless in the behaviour, beliefs and very existence of this new breed. Most of them could not afford to live in Dublin 4 and, being intensely aware of the political implications, would rather die than admit to doing so. Nevertheless, the geographical area of Dublin 4 was pertinent to the philosophical mind-set, in much the same way as the hole in the middle is an intrinsic part of a Polo mint. The area of Dublin 4 itself, as well as the extended spiritual hinterland covering much of the southside, had about it many of the qualities of a country village. It formed the new centre of a city rapidly tilting in a southward direction. For those reared to an urban sensibility in any part of the country, it became a home away from home. It had all the advantages of the places in which they had grown up, and yet hardly any of the disadvantages. After a few visits to a particular shop or pub, for example, you came to be recognised and spoken to on first-name terms. And yet there was no hierarchy to put you in your place. Here was a place in which you could reinvent yourself in the image not of your background or your family but of your ideal self. This was a place in which the fantasy you lived in your head could become reality. It was possible to live your life between your home, your place of work, a small handful of pubs, one or two theatres and cinemas, and a few restaurants and coffee shops, without being any more than vaguely aware of the other Dublin on the fringes.

There were those in Dublin still sufficiently detached from this new class to see that, by monopolising the country's means of talking to itself, the people of 'Dublin 4' were well advanced in a process of marginalising the majority experience. They had become adept not just at imposing their view of Ireland on the country at large, but at removing from sight all evidence that things had ever been different.

'Dublin 4' was an attitude of mind, an attitude that had become impatient with the reality of life in modern Ireland. There were those who held that the term defined a class of people who regarded themselves as the social and intellectual elite of modern Ireland, but who ideally would have liked to have been born somewhere else. Others saw 'Dublin 4' as a new bourgeoisie, a class of people who had transcended their own class and background, who were out to culturally colonise the country, who believed themselves to have an almost divine right to dictate the way it should be run. The 'Dublin 4' animal was polished and cosmopolitan, though not necessarily as privileged as the leafy avenues of Ballsbridge might lead the outsider to believe. It wanted no truck with the dark, irrational, priest-ridden place it called 'rural Ireland'. For 'Dublin 4', this place was just a bad dream, a mild irritation on the periphery of its consciousness, a darkness on the edge of town. It wanted an end to all this fanciful talk about an attachment to the land. It wanted Ireland to see itself as a modern, urban, industrialised democracy.

In time, both 'Dublin 4' and what it described as 'rural Ireland' became mutually reinforcing stereotypes, one depending on the other for affirmation. It is in the nature of stereotypes to be self-fulfilling, to take root in the fertile ground of mutual suspicion. The new tribe defined Ireland on radio and television, the old listened with growing incomprehension to this strange definition of the country it had imagined itself to inhabit. It was a perfect new tribal division for a people in love with tribal warfare.

'Dublin 4' was itself a republic of the mind, a mind that had decided that the rest of the country had lagged behind. This was a generation that had been reared to the promise of an Ireland free from the grip of history and religion. To an extent, this Ireland had already been brought about in the imagination of 'Dublin 4'. All that was required was for the rest of the population to agree to lie down and die.

But ultimately, if we were honest, 'Dublin 4' was a part of all of us: the part of our brains that wanted Ireland to be different, better, that wanted to walk through agreeable, leafy streets with blinkers carefully adjusted. It was the part of us which refused to face up to ourselves as we were. We all needed some escape from reality, but in the creation of a whole section of society that had allowed this tendency to dominate its thinking there was scope for seriously deluding ourselves.

11

The Inside of Two Rooms

It is hard for someone who has just come up from Roscommon to grasp the fact that the 'Dublin' they have become aware of from radio and television is, in fact, a much smaller place than the one they have just left. The reason this is so is that, by and large, the people who generate modern Ireland's conversation with itself are known to each other, in much the same way as people from opposite ends of a small town might say of each other, 'Yes, I know him.' The notion of Dublin as a city of over a million people is therefore misleading. People who are involved in public life in the broadest sense – that is, people in politics, the financial and legal professions, the media, and others of the class that are in positions to make themselves the opinion-formers of Irish society – have a much greater chance of running into one another within their social circle in Dublin than, for example, two pensioners from different sides of Ballaghaderreen going in on a Friday to collect their pensions. The stretch of Dublin's thoroughfare from the Shelbourne Hotel on St Stephen's Green to Jury's Hotel in Ballsbridge, wherein takes place much of the loose talk that will forge Ireland's future image of itself, is about a mile long.

I soon found myself working along this stretch. For all sorts of reasons I was no longer comfortable with just writing for *Hot Press*. I felt it an increasingly inadequate vehicle for expressing the ambiguous feelings I had about my new surroundings. At home I had been an outsider, but here I was acutely conscious that I was an outsider as well, that I belonged not to Dublin but definitively to Castlerea. As an outsider in Roscommon, *Hot Press* had given me a means of expression which connected me to the outside, but as an outsider in Dublin I found it to be an integral part of a consensus of which I was increasingly suspicious – the consensus of Dublin 4.

The magazine I wanted to write for was *Magill*. This was the creation of a strange and enigmatic man named Vincent Browne, who had founded it in 1977 more or less as a weapon for hitting politicians across the head. Browne, then in his early forties, had come from Broadford, County Limerick, and was regarded as the most brilliant journalist of his generation. From 1977 to 1983, he had published and edited *Magill* from a poky office on Merrion Row. His comprehensive articles on the background to the Arms Trial, on its tenth anniversary in 1980, had led him to become a household name. My father thought he was wonderful and agreed with almost everything he said.

Month after month in his magazine, Browne heaped abuse upon the heads of the politicians whom he accused of misruling the country. The covers of *Magill* were always brave and startling. 'Arms Crisis 1970: The Inside Story', 'How Charlie Cooked the Books', 'Charles Haughey: Immobilised by Indecision', 'The Politicians have

Vandalised the Country'. For the first time, it seemed, here was someone who was not taking sides, who had the same exceedingly dim view of all politicians.

For years in Castlerea, on the first Thursday of every month, I could not wait to get up to Mulvihill's to buy the latest *Magill*. Sometimes, if their copies were delayed or mislaid, I would drive the eighteen miles to Roscommon to buy the magazine.

About a year previously, in the spring of 1983, Browne had ceased editing *Magill* to start his own Sunday newspaper, the resurrected *Sunday Tribune*. In his seat at *Magill* was a man named Colm Tóibín, who like myself had come up from the country, from Enniscorthy, County Wexford. He had arrived in Dublin in the early seventies, to study at UCD and later had begun working as a journalist with *In Dublin* magazine, of which he had subsequently become features editor. This magazine came out once a fortnight and could not be bought in Castlerea; but every second Thursday, during Tóibín's period as editor, I had driven to Roscommon to buy a copy.

On finishing college in 1975, Tóibín had spent a couple of years in Spain. His arrival there had coincided with the death of Franco, and his witnessing of the country's transition from dictatorship to constitutional monarchy had had a profound effect on his view of politics. When he returned to Ireland, he saw Irish politicians anew, and wrote of them as strange creatures inhabiting a weird and fantastic landscape. Some of his articles were just plain torrents of abuse, witty and colloquial, against politicians and other public figures. Others contained a vast amount of information and insight, carefully woven into a narrative that was far from the deadened prose of much journalism of the time. When he wrote, he seemed to go beyond the mere recounting of factual information, to give some sense of the mystery, the complexity of much to do with modern Irish politics. In many ways he was a better editor of *Magill* than Browne had been. He appeared to have less of an urge to bring down the government each month, but then, despite Browne's best efforts, governments and politicians just went their own way. Tóibín's style was less cataclysmic, but in a quiet way his sabre seemed to draw more blood. He was the kind of journalist I wanted to be. He was a day younger than I was.

I met Tóibín by accident and we got on quite well. When I first met him, I imagined that he looked much older than I did. He had longish hair but was balding at the front. His beard was bushy and unkempt, and most of his front teeth were missing. He had read several of my articles in *Hot Press* and had liked something about them; he thought they were funny, but told me that parts of them did not ring true. He had noticed the things about them that had bothered me, the things that I had clouded in ambiguity by putting words into the mouth of Cryptic Jim. Tóibín, I noticed, had his own ways of protecting himself. He seemed to have absorbed innumerable personae he had observed in Enniscorthy, and used their idiosyncrasies to cover his tracks. I noticed too that, like me, he had a lot of self-doubts and confusions. He did not appear to be at home in Dublin. 'Dublin for me,' he would say, 'is the inside of two rooms.' He had his ways, too, of distracting attention from his own insecurities. In the company of certain people he appeared uncomfortable with having come from 'the country', and the nearest available culchie would become the butt of his jokes: 'John, of course, is up from the country'; 'John, of course, hasn't been to university. And it sometimes shows, I'm afraid.' His every utterance, no matter how ostensibly vicious, was clothed in irony. 'Nobody,' he once told me, 'will ever know what I really think.' He wanted to be a writer, a 'proper writer' as he would say, as opposed to a mere journalist. This, too, you imagined, was ironic, for Tóibín did not seem to believe that journalism was in any way an inferior form. He would talk lovingly about a particular article someone had written, of the beauty of the language, of what they had written, quoting whole sections he had learned by heart.

Tóibín was afraid of his life of Vincent Browne and made no attempt to deny it. The week he had taken the job as editor of *Magill*, he had written in *In Dublin* that Browne was 'erratic and pig-headed', and he had never been given any reason to change his opinion. In the evenings in O'Donoghue's pub, next door to the *Magill* offices, he would talk of his latest encounter with his employer. He would describe their weekly meetings, which he said were like having a double-science class at school. He hated science and said that the mere thought of the weekly double-science used to spoil three days of his week.

Browne's reputation for truculence among his employees somewhat belied his cuddly public image. On the TV screen, talking about the wrongdoings of politicians, he was curly-haired and cleverly ironic. It was not until afterwards, when I myself worked for Browne, that Tóibín's descriptions began to make sense.

Browne was undoubtedly one of the most brilliant and extraordinary people I had ever encountered. Like most people he had his quotas of good and bad qualities, but in him they seemed to be more polarised than is normal. He had a remarkable capacity for personal generosity, was utterly unimpressed by class, education or qualifications, and was encouraging of people in whom he detected a glimmer of like-mindedness. At all times he appeared brimful of energy, ideas and devastating logic. It was as though anything his gigantic ego brought its gaze upon would immediately become possible. But this, too, had its downside, and Browne also possessed qualities which made him a difficult employer. He had, through the force of his personality, created a whole new model of Irish journalism, and often seemed to be intent upon dismantling it again. Everyone wanted to work for him, but dozens failed in the attempt, unable to stand his moods and his extraordinary capacity for aggravation. With his passion and dynamism he sucked people in and then, as often as not, would tire of them and drive them away through the sheer brunt of his hostility. One man who had worked for him said that the secret of Browne's success was that his destructiveness was just about outweighed by his charisma; it's about the closest anyone has come to summing him up. He was extremely entertaining company, but was utterly unpredictable. He could turn from persuasiveness to unpleasantness as though by throwing a switch. He seemed to mistrust order, calm and organisation, to thrive on crisis and chaos. He was gregarious and enjoyed company, but like a jealous lover, was often most threatened by the people he liked most. Ultimately, it did not seem to matter to him what others thought about him. *Magill* was an extension of his personality, and he could not bear to see it thrive in the care of someone else, particularly if that person happened to be in love with it as well. He created it, he would admit later, as a stepping-stone to his own Sunday newspaper, but even after he had achieved his objective, could never bring himself to leave it behind. I would be one of half a dozen people who would edit *Magill*, for ever-diminishing periods, between his departure as editor in 1983 and the demise of the magazine seven years later, but in effect he remained the editor throughout. Ideally he would have wanted an editor without any personality with which to infect his magazine.

For these and other reasons, once behind the closed doors of *Magill*, Vincent's cuddliness very often evaporated. He seemed to use the magazine as a way of relieving the frustrations of editing the *Sunday Tribune*. Editorial meetings would begin in a mood of mere impatience: he hadn't liked this or that in the latest issue of the magazine; he didn't want this taken the wrong way, but really you could not say such and such in this magazine – it just wasn't that kind of magazine. He would pick up a copy of *Magill* and leaf through its pages with escalating annoyance. Finally he would cast it from him. 'It's shite,' he would declare. The editor then would be asked to explain how come the magazine was 'shite'. If a satisfactory explanation was not forthcoming, Browne would launch into a tirade of abuse, always ending in the same manner. 'What worries me is not that the magazine is so bad. It's that you don't seem to know how bad it is.'

What Browne appeared to hate most about his magazine while Tóibín was editor was its irrationality. However, the articles in any given issue were almost invariably better than those in the issues that Browne himself had edited, and many were far superior. Apart from Tóibín himself, there was Gene Kerrigan, a brilliant and highly individualistic journalist who wrote about Ireland from the perspective of a northside-born Dubliner. Browne had discovered him, but it was since Tóibín's arrival that Kerrigan had really begun to bloom.

There was another element that the magazine had not possessed under Browne. It was something intangible, something that told the reader things which the words in their literal meanings did not convey. There was something about the tone, about how the magazine was put together, which made you feel that one Thursday you might buy it and be told what it was about this country and what you were doing here.

Browne, as I subsequently learned from working for him, hated any hint of irrationality, despite the fact that he was himself one of the most irrational people I had ever met. He believed that anything could be learned or explained by the harvesting of facts and their tabulation in a particular sequence. He seemed, as one journalist noted, to have an almost sexual hunger to find out things. He wanted to know what everybody in the public eye was doing with their time, how much they were being paid, and whether they were giving us value for money.

For years, the monthly planning meetings in *Magill* were distributed with lists of stories to be attempted, the first of which was, 'Charlie Haughey's money'. From time to time, someone would volunteer, or be browbeaten into volunteering, to attempt this story. The result would always be the same. After weeks of research, they would come back and report that nobody was able to say how much money Charlie Haughey had, never mind how he had acquired it. Browne would interrogate them rigorously, often flying into a rage of frustration. Had they tried such and such? Perhaps so and so knew something? In the end it would come to nothing, but this 'story' would stay at the top of the list. Browne genuinely believed that the mystery of Charlie Haughey and his hold on the Irish people could be unravelled by such methods, and he was deeply suspicious of journalists who did not seem to share this belief.

Although he did much to encourage young journalists, Browne was suspicious of journalists who were good writers. He seemed to believe that they attempted to conceal their lack of research, the fact that they had been unable to obtain any new information, behind literary style or personal opinions. Some journalists would keep souvenirs of memos Browne had written for stories he had commissioned them to do. Sometimes he would put at the end, 'No "Writing", and no opinions'.

But Browne always got his way, and in the spring of 1985 Tóibín left *Magill*, unable to take any more. The magazine returned to being rational, occasionally getting the 'goods' on a politician, but for the most part receding into indifference. The newspapers borrowed the best of what *Magill* had shown journalism should do. They began to carry better written articles, but nevertheless these lacked the mystery and excitement of Tóibín's *Magill*. They were rational, fair and objective. Tóibín, too, changed after *Magill*. He no longer spoke excitedly about the promise of journalism. He was shattered by his loss of the magazine, almost as another might have been by the loss of a great love. He put his energy and his mystery into the writing of a novel. Tóibín still wrote articles, but he wrote them more quickly now, and made no secret of the fact that he was writing them for the money. Many great writers, he would say, had been hacks on the side.

Tóibín had been unable to give me any work at *Magill*, but through his intercession I was granted an interview with Browne, which offered the prospect of freelance work with the *Sunday Tribune*. He was as nice as pie, much more pleasant than I had been led to believe. He made jokes, his mouth curling with irony whenever he was especially pleased with one of his utterances. I had brought along a bundle of clippings of my work for *Hot Press*. He read them all, slowly and carefully. For a whole half-hour he said nothing, while I stared out of the window, pretending to study the flight patterns of the swooping crows outside. At last he looked up, his features knitted into a puzzled frown. He stared at me hard and quizzically from underneath his bushy eyebrows. 'Who the fuck,' he asked, 'is Cryptic Jim?'

12

The Lords of the DANSE

A short walk from the *Magill* office was Doheny & Nesbitt's. In the same way as phrases like 'national handlers' and 'Dublin 4' had entered the political language of the time, so this pub had given its name to a particular brand of economic thinking. The Doheny and Nesbitt School of Economics was first named, half in jest, by Dick Walsh, political editor of the *Irish Times*, and the appellation quickly caught on as a way of summing up a set of views on the Irish economy which was rapidly gaining a firm foothold within the political system.

Throughout the seventies, Doheny & Nesbitt's had been a poky, smoky little pub with a minimum of creature comforts, frequented by students and civil servants from one or other of the government departments situated on nearby Merrion Street. The pub had been taken over some years previously by the Tipperary-born partnership of Ned Doheny and Tom Nesbitt, who, after serving an apprenticeship in the bar trade in Dublin, went to America for several years to make the price of a pub. The story of how their pub became a centre of economic thinking is part truth and part wishful thinking.

In the mid-seventies, the story goes, there was a barman by the name of Niall Fleming, who worked in Madigan's pub in Donnybrook, then the favourite haunt of RTE staff, particularly journalists and producers. During one of the lengthy bank strikes of the seventies, Fleming made a lot of friends among the RTE people by being especially obliging in cashing their paycheques in the bar till. So fond did they become of him, in fact, that when he changed jobs to a pub in Upper Baggot Street, many of them made his new pub their regular. However, the place did not prove to their liking in other respects, and gradually they began to move away in ones and twos, trying out new pubs in the neighbourhood, now that they had ventured into town. Eventually, more and more of them began to congregate in Doheny & Nesbitt's, a place that fulfilled their notion of what a pub should be.

For sheer lack of money, the owners had never got around to refurbishing the pub, as they had planned, as a modern lounge bar. The interior was as it had been for over a century: wooden partitions, a couple of hideaway snugs, a stone floor, very little lighting and the most basic of barstools. This, oddly enough, was precisely how the new clientele liked their pubs to be.

Up until then, journalists from the various newspapers had tended towards clannishness, each keeping to pubs close to their own newspaper offices. But now they began to gravitate towards 'Nesbitt's', as the pub became known. As time went by, the crowd expanded to embrace larger numbers from the civil service, from the legal and other professions, as well as certain leading politicians. Also regularly present was a small group of economists, who talked a lot about the state of the national economy and football. Three men seemed to be present more often than others: Paul Tansey, the economics correspondent of the *Irish Times*, Sean Barrett, a lecturer in economics at Trinity College, and Colm McCarthy, the 'Dean' of the Doheny and Nesbitt School of Economics (DANSE), who had worked with the Central Bank and the Economic and Social Research Institute.

The politics of the group embraced almost the entire spectrum, but they were agreed on one thing: since the adoption of deficit budgeting as an economic strategy in the seventies, Irish politicians had become increasingly reckless and had allowed the public finances to go out of control. Almost all the gang had been educated in the Keynesian school of economics at UCD, but the oil crisis of 1973 had cast a deep shadow over Keynesian economic thinking. The worldwide recession of the late seventies had taught economists to be suspicious of the belief that governments could control and manipulate the economy by using budget deficits to counter cyclical trends. The group had had their thinking radicalised by this experience and had come to favour, to different degrees, the recently fashionable monetarist economics championed in particular by the American Milton Friedman.

It was sometime in 1980 that Vincent Browne first came across the Lords of the DANSE. They had already begun to feed their views into the public consciousness via the *Irish Times*, but it was Browne who put them centrestage. He was deeply hostile to the notion of politics as something separate from the running of the country. Because he came from a small town in County Limerick, he had an acute understanding of the nature of country-cute politicians.

Browne told stories of the crookedness and cunning of such politicians with great relish. He was a marvellous mimic and was capable of reducing an entire pub to helpless laughter with a send-up of Gerry Collins, who represented Browne's home constituency of Limerick West. But his liking and enjoyment of politicians seemed to run parallel to his passion for finding them out in some wrongdoing, for blowing the whistle, for making them, as he would pronounce grandly in his editorials, 'accountable' for their actions.

Although he knew almost nothing about economics, Browne quickly recognised that this was not just a perfect issue for censuring politicians, but was also one with enormous potential for catching the public imagination. His last major splash in *Magill* had been the replay of the 1970 Arms Crisis, which had broken all records for Irish magazine sales. But a year or so later, after a number of indifferent issues, things were beginning to go off the boil. Over the coming months, *Magill* carried an occasional series of articles on the state of the economy, some written by members of the DANSE, others by Browne himself. In January 1982, he appeared on *The Late Late Show*, berating a panel of politicians for their mishandling of the country's finances. I remember coming in and seeing my father watching him carefully. 'He's a smart fellow, that Browne,' he said.

Browne was far smarter than any of the others who came to be associated with the Doheny and Nesbitt School of Economics. They were putty in his hands. Within a couple of years, people on street corners were loudly accusing politicians of vandalising the country. Gay Byrne was on the radio, day in and day out, denouncing politicians for being useless, for being overpaid, for not giving value for their wages. Suddenly it seemed that a new rationalism was sweeping the country; people were beginning to make an imaginative connection between the act of voting and the quality of political life. The notion of politics as a sort of historical blood sport was being challenged for the first time.

Following Tóibín's departure in 1985, the sales of *Magill* had begun to decline yet again. It was believed, especially by Vincent himself, that this was because he was no longer editing the magazine. But perhaps the real reason was that the ideas *Magill* had done so much to make palatable had soured on the tongue of a public which by now was over-dosing on Dublin 4 outrage.

It was around this time, funnily enough, that in faraway Roscommon, I noticed the radio becoming increasingly shrill. The economists from the Doheny and Nesbitt School came on to join the parade of progressives and constitutional crusaders to admonish the public for 'living beyond its means'. They intoned terms like Gross National Product, devaluation, spiralling inflation, and buoyancy. They gave out about the nature of Irish political culture and accused people of living in 'cloud cuckoo land'. They spoke, too, about 'white elephants' – developments that had been put in place by politicians for, they said, entirely electoral reasons. It was remarked from time to time that they were extremely selective about these. Knock Airport was one – the airport on a 'foggy boggy hill' – but Dublin's new electric railway system, which connected some of the most affluent areas of Dublin to the city centre, was not. They were attacking not just politics but also the people who elected these politicians. It was as though they had decided that the country outside Dublin was a millstone around the neck of the capital. If we did not have all these mucksavages to contend with, maybe we could have a decent standard of living.

The people of Ireland began to turn down their radios. And, oddly enough, Vincent Browne stopped drinking in Doheny & Nesbitt's. Several years later, I would volunteer the subject as a suitable one for an article in *Magill*. By this time, the 'Dean' of the DANSE, Colm McCarthy, who had previously been close to Fine Gael's John Bruton, was a paid adviser to the Fianna Fáil government. With two senior civil servants, he was sitting daily in a conference room in the Department of Finance, discussing where public expenditure cuts should be made. Back in Nesbitt's, this group became known as An Bord Snip.

Browne was enthusiastic about every aspect of the story, except the question of his own involvement. He wrote me a long memo, detailing what he believed to be the most important aspects: 'Do a bit about how many of them are now spokespeople for a very wealthy class, having joined the financial services.' Browne stressed that he no longer drank in Nesbitt's because he found the DANSE people boring:

On the whole and in many cases individually they are a terrible pain in the ass. They think they have the answer to everything. They also think they are very funny . . . They are tickled to death simply by meeting people they otherwise deride – for instance they get so chuffed if Charlie speaks to them. They rush around to Doheny's to tell the others all about it, and what brilliant witticism they said back etc. Pathetic really . . . They also love to go on television and they will tell you again and again how clever and witty they were and how foolish they made others look and all that . . . None of these fellows gives a bugger about anyone who is poor . . . Anyway, how all these codgers hijacked the Irish establishment is a good story, and in particular how they put the dampers on Haughey in the past fifteen months.

I asked him about his own part in allowing these codgers to hijack the establishment, but he denied it utterly. He had a way of denying things that made you believe, for a short period and in all sincerity, that you had made a mistake. He had certainly highlighted the view of those concerned about the way the economy was being run, he admitted, but he had always tempered this view with an insistence that the weaker sections of society should not be made victims of the economic knife.

It struck me that what Browne was asking me to do was to write a version of the story without him in it, to enter it into history as though it had had nothing to do with him. The reason, I believed, was that although the Dublin 4 conventional wisdom of the time saw the DANSE influence as one of the great successes for rationalism over the political culture of the country, Browne himself saw it as a failure. A movement that had been started with a much broader agenda had been hijacked by a group of individuals with a narrower focus. They were one-trick ponies: they knew nothing about much except economics and football. The economy might have been sorted out for the moment, but the nation was still trammelled in the embrace of the irrational. What worried Browne about the DANSE people was not that things were bad, but that they did not understand just how bad things were.

13

Gaybo's Fault Again

Although he would never countenance having a television set in the house while we were growing up, my father would often go out to the house of his friend, Ned Rock, the shoemaker who lived up the street, to watch *The Late Late Show*. For days afterwards he would fulminate about 'that bowsie Byrne', or about something that someone called Ulick O'Connor had said.

By the time we got a television set, *The Late Late* had ceased to be as important as everyone was always saying it was, though from time to time it would come alive with a discussion on some aspect of Irish life, and ensure a captive audience for its indifferent output over the next couple of months.

It was on radio that Gay Byrne's influence was greatest. His was the most consistently authentic voice to emerge from the tribal drum and resonate through the echo chamber of the entire society. This may have had something to do with the fact that he spent most of his summer holidays with his family in a cottage in Donegal. My father never listened to Gay Byrne on the radio, except when he was unable to avoid it, and even then his face would glaze over with indifference. If he had listened more, I often thought, he might have got to quite like it, in the same way as he had slowly allowed himself to be won over by *Coronation Street* and *Glenroe*. What I think he objected to most about Byrne was his instinct for entertainment – the apparent need he had to turn every item on *The Late Late* into a piece of cabaret. He did this much less on the radio.

On his radio show, there was a clear delineation between entertainment and seriousness. He was a master of tone and mood. On *The Late Late*, the pendulum swung between narrowly placed stays, but on the radio it swung freely. There was no level of intensity it did not seem capable of reaching. Sometimes, if you were parked in your car in town, you would see people driving past, in stitches at the same joke that you yourself were laughing at. But there were a few occasions in the first half of the 1980s when the expressions on their faces were likely to be rather more subdued.

A number of incidents which occurred in this period caused Gay Byrne to pull out all the stops, and do what he did best. One was the case of Eileen Flynn, the County Wexford teacher who had been dismissed from her job when she became pregnant by a man with whom she was living who was separated from his wife. Another was the case of Ann Lovett, the Granard girl who died giving birth in a grotto. He would introduce such subjects well into the show, probably after the ten o'clock news; the jokes, quips and funny voices would have gone, and he would introduce the subject in calm, measured tones. He would give no warning and make no apology. In the case of Ann

Lovett, he spent an entire programme reading out letters he had got from listeners, alternating with an actress in reading the letters. Both read dispassionately and evenly, without drama. The country shivered and went silent.

Gay Byrne gave the impression of being highly opinionated, but nobody really knew what he thought about anything. Sometimes when he seemed to be delivering pronouncements, he was merely acting as a lubricant, oiling the wheels of the debate, taking both sides of the argument at once. He had occasionally, however, admitted to having a sneaking admiration for Charlie Haughey.

If *The Late Late* was a spectacle, a cabaret-style entertainment, the radio show was altogether more complex: it was a mirror which a large part of Irish society held up to itself each morning, a forum in which ordinary people became involved in whatever was the current debate. This was perhaps the one forum on Irish radio in the eighties which did not belong to Dublin 4.

But there was one issue on which Gay Byrne did appear to have very definite opinions. He believed, as he kept saying throughout much of the eighties, that the country was 'banjaxed', and talked about this day after day, accusing politicians of incompetence, stupidity and corruption. He fed intravenously into the Irish consciousness the notion that politicians were all on the make, that they were in it for what they could get out of it, that they were all the same. Sometimes a politician would ring in to accuse him of being unfair and he would hit back by accusing the politician of using his show to get publicity. As time went on, Byrne became more and more impatient, as though he suspected that nothing would ever change. In the end he was advising people who had a choice in the matter to leave the country and start up somewhere else. Occasionally he would do special programmes on Australia and how to get there, or America and how to go about obtaining a visa.

Gay Byrne seemed increasingly tired of the past; he became dismissive of people who were not as fed up with it as he was, who trotted out the old shibboleths which he detested. It was said that a lot of his ill-feeling towards politicians stemmed from his personal financial situation. He had had his life's savings taken by an accountant who had also been his best friend, and he was working all hours to try to make up for the loss. But the tax system, as he continuously pointed out, made it impossible to make money, no matter how hard you worked.

Just before Christmas 1987, I went to meet Gay Byrne to interview him for *In Dublin*, of which I was then the editor. For background material, I sat in on what turned out to be a run-of-the-mill programme, the likes of which I had listened to on many mornings as I drove the green Hiace around County Roscommon. In my article, I described the flesh-and-blood presence behind the voice that had so often scratched the complacency of the country, and which had uttered so many words in trying to make us forget the past:

In Studio Five of the Radio Centre, Gay Byrne is seated at the desk in the inner studio chamber. He is running through the various scripts for the day, reading them aloud, pitching them, timing them, changing the odd little detail here and there. His hands are clasped in front of him and from the control booth outside it appears as though he is praying. His expression is businesslike, full of concentration, but when the red light goes on in a few minutes he will be like a man transformed: smiling, grimacing, pouting, grinning, exactly as he appears on television. He will act out every letter, every snippet from the papers, as though the audience could see as well as hear him.

When the show began, Byrne went through several items before he came to what had become his favourite theme. He referred to an article in that morning's *Irish Independent*, under the headline, 'Gloomy Gay Fails to Keep Our Spirits Up'. 'A leading psychologist' had criticised Gay Byrne for 'adding to the underlying mood of pessimism in the country', taking him severely to task for advising young people to leave Ireland. Such comments on a highly influential radio show, the psychologist said, would only aggravate matters.

'Now,' said Byrne to his microphone, 'I see they're at me again. I'm the one who's causing the gloom, doom and depression in the country. I suppose I'm the one who's responsible for the 300,000 unemployed in the country. It's my fault that the streets of London, New York and Frankfurt are lined with young, Irish, well-educated adults. It's Gaybo's fault again. The country is in a poor financial and economic state. But you, the listeners to this programme, could be forgiven for being far more pessimistic because of my comments. It's Gaybo's fault again.' Later that day, the *Evening Herald* carried a front-page story about Gay Byrne 'hitting back' at his critic. Most listeners would believe that Gay Byrne had got up that morning and, on reading the morning paper, had decided to 'hit back' at the psychologist who had attacked him. This was Gay Byrne giving it to them hard. This was the real Gay Byrne, the one who had changed the face of modern Ireland.

The trouble was that, while I was listening to Gay Byrne delivering his script with measured annoyance, I could not get out of my head the image of his producer, John Caden, dictating that exact script to a secretary in my presence at 8.30 that morning. Whoever this 'Gay Byrne' was, he was much more than the man sitting in the chair at the microphone who looked so like him. And whatever this Gay Byrne made the people of Ireland feel, it was not certain whether or not he shared their feelings.

14

The Steak Story

The country defined itself, was defined, by its relationship with Charles Haughey. You could not be neutral: you could be for him, you could be against him, or you could be ambiguous about him. There were journalists who had built careers out of their loyalty or loathing for him. New words and phrases were constantly being coined in the newspapers to mock or honour him: GUBU, The Golden Boy, The Great National Bastard. Even those who hated him appeared to be obsessed with him, with convincing others that he was an unsuitable person to lead the country, with hoping to see him removed from the possibility of office once and for all. I preferred to be ambiguous. That way, you could be ambiguously for or ambiguously against him.

I remember the morning I first read the word GUBU. I was sitting in the Hiace on the outskirts of Ballinagare, trying to kill time. It was about 7.30 and I wasn't due at the post office in Ballinagare until 7.45. I read Conor Cruise O'Brien's column in that morning's *Irish Times*, in which he poked fun at Charles Haughey's latest disaster.

A man wanted for murder had been found hiding in the house of the Fianna Fáil government's Attorney General. It was one of those coincidences which occur all the time in ordinary life but which should not happen to great leaders. Mr Haughey had described the incident as 'grotesque, unbelievable, bizarre and unprecedented'. Conor Cruise O'Brien, one of those who had built a career out of a deep and very special loathing for Haughey, had that morning coined the acronym GUBU, to describe this and other accidents that had developed a habit of happening to Mr Haughey. I sat in the van by the side of the road and laughed and laughed. Oddly enough, I never afterwards heard the word used by anybody who was not either a journalist or a political activist from a party other than Fianna Fáil, but the word had caught on in Dublin, or at least in media circles and within the psychic and geographical territory of Dublin 4.

It was almost an article of faith among journalists and other citizens of Dublin 4 that Haughey was the anti-Christ. If such an opinion was canvassed in your presence and you did not immediately concur, a rumour might grow that you were secretly a Hagheyite. If this rumour got to the ears of commissioning editors, you were unlikely to be asked to write about politics.

And yet, writing about Irish politics in the 1980s meant writing about Charles Haughey. His face on a magazine cover meant that the magazine would sell. Of no other politician of the time could this so definitively be stated. In this same period, only one other Irish politician approached Haughey's selling power, and that was Sean Doherty.

One of the main reasons that I always preferred magazine journalism was that it seemed to live longer than any other form. This was not because I wanted my own work immortalised, but because only in this way did the past continue to be believable. History books were dead things, full of dates and chronologies, in which there was rarely a hint that the people these things had happened to were in any respect like real people. The sound of voices on the radio disappeared into thin air, the flitting images of history unfolding on television were emblematic of the way politicians flitted in and out of our consciousness; but, once broadcast, these pictures were hardly ever seen again. If occasionally they were, they somehow contrived to appear as though they had originated in a different place, a place more innocent, less cynical than this. Everyone seemed fatter, or thinner, or had more hair than you remembered. It was as if all these things had happened to a different people, who lived somewhere else.

Newspapers did not keep: they faded and turned brown. Reading them was like watching a black-and-white movie; you imagined that the world they described had been brown and dog-eared as well. Even as you read them on the day of publication, you could not escape this thought: that the world you were reading about already was slipping from your grasp. As though to counteract this, newspaper journalists couched their recordings of events in a language they had created especially for this purpose; a language rendered dead by their attempts to make it live for ever, a language stifled by its own urge for immortality.

Magazines, somehow, had avoided this trap. With *Magill*, Vincent Browne had created not just a different kind of journalistic outlet, but a different medium, a new way of colouring in the unwinding of history. Through the influence of people like Colm Tóibín, the language of the magazines of the time was sharp and alive. Moreover, magazines, unlike newspapers, had all the tactile qualities of literature: the words on their pages seemed to be preserved in a form that still seemed true years after the event. They could be kept under the stairs and taken out when the country's memory began to play tricks. They were history taken alive. They would grow into neat piles of the past.

As with the country at large, periodicals of the time came to be defined through their attitude to Haughey. Each month, each fortnight, the same face gazed out from the shelves of the country's newsagents. The headlines seemed carefully chosen to suit the changing demeanour of the face: ANYTHING IS BETTER THAN CHARLIE HAUGHEY. THE PRICE OF HAUGHEY'S RETURN TO POWER. HAUGHEY IN DISTRESS. ARE WE GOING TO HAVE CHARLIE HAUGHEY TO KICK AROUND ANYMORE? THE LAST DAYS OF CHARLIE HAUGHEY. THE MOST EXTRAORDINARY CHARLES J. HAUGHEY INTERVIEW EVER. HOW CHARLIE WON THE WAR. NOTHING COULD BE WORSE THAN CHARLIE HAUGHEY.

Haughey had become a mystery of his own creation. He seemed to have decided that in Irish politics it was not enough to be loved; you had to be hated as well. He would be the fat chieftain. The people who loved you needed others to hate you so that they could fan the flames of their love in the cold blasts of the prevailing winds of contempt. This, in my view, was the key to his success, to his seemingly indestructible belief in his destiny as leader of the Irish people.

As though to goad his detractors, he would indulge in extravagant, vain gestures, like the time he brought out a book of his speeches amounting to over 1,200 pages. It was the kind of book you could put behind a door in a storm and, no matter how it blowed and blowed, the door would not be budged. I was editor of *In Dublin* at the time, and asked the socialist Noel Browne, a politician who had only ever managed to be loved, to review the book. He sent it back, begging to be excused. I told him that he did not actually have to read it: 'Just put it on the mantelpiece and look at it,' I said. A fortnight later he delivered a review of the book, which summed up better than had ever been done the problem which so many people had with Charles Haughey. We put Noel Browne on the cover for a change; he was the only Irish politician you could put on the cover and have people buy the magazine for utterly positive reasons.

Browne wrote beautifully, which is to say that he was a man who knew that meaning was not conveyed by words alone. There was a magic in his every sentence, the possibility of the unexpected, a transcendence of the everyday. He was not afraid of showing anger. The book, he said, reflected 'the egomaniacal self-image of a profoundly insecure, troubled personality, desperately needing public reassurance'. Haughey, he wrote, 'needs adulation and admiration as the rest of us need oxygen'. What the book proved above all, in Browne's opinion, was that Haughey's drive for power had been carefully orchestrated. Browne referred to some of the speeches he had forced himself to read: speeches about the Irish people's 'deep sense of the religious', Haughey's belief in capitalism, his rejection of socialism. He referred to Haughey's flaunting of his own vast wealth, 'as though to mock the unemployed and hungry'. But, he declared, 'Haughey's millions, together with his estates and mansion, are no substitute for the ego-juice of standing ovations and the harsh lights of the election rooms and television studios. Haughey represents a new breed of politician, who must have position rather than power. Past experience as Minister for Finance, Agriculture, Justice, Health and even Taoiseach itself, shows that Haughey derives his greatest pleasure, paradoxically, from refusing to exercise his power for the benefit of society.'

These views, less eloquently put, were the stuff of many public house conversations in the official Dublin at that time. At night after work, in the upstairs lounge of O'Donoghue's, journalists from *Magill*, *In Dublin*, *Hot Press* and the *Sunday Tribune* would meet. Much of the talk would be about Haughey. Coming up to Christmas 1984, I was on the promise of an interview with him, to be published in *Hot Press*. Everyone was full of suggestions about questions I should ask. 'Ask him about his money. Where did he make his money?' 'There's no point: he'll just tell you to fuck off.' 'Ask him about the Arms Trial.' 'Sure! Then you're really fucked.'

Colm Tóibín was adamant that I should use the article in *Hot Press* to tell the Steak Story. This story had been told to him by a friend, who some years before had worked in the kitchens of a hotel down the country. The hotel was occasionally visited by Charles Haughey and his entourage while he was on the chicken and chips circuit in the late 1970s, working up support for his approaching bid for the Fianna Fáil leadership. The chef in the hotel loathed Charles Haughey with a special passion.

When Haughey would come into the hotel's restaurant, the chef would peep out from behind the kitchen door and rub his hands in gleeful anticipation. Haughey always had steak, so the chef would proceed to select the biggest and best steak in the kitchen.

When the waiter came in from taking the order at Haughey's table, he would duly confirm that Mr Haughey had indeed ordered a large, medium-rare steak. The ritual would then follow an established pattern. The chef would take the steak in one hand and unbutton his trousers with the other. Then he would put the steak down into his underpants and begin to rub the meat on his penis and testicles. He would do this, slowly and deliberately, for a minute or more. Then he would take the steak from his private parts and place it on the pan. When cooked, it would be served up to Mr Haughey, whom the chef would observe while he was eating. Always the waiter would come back in to convey Mr Haughey's 'compliments to the chef'. Everyone would almost die from laughing, as would the entire bar in O'Donoghue's when the story was retold.

I had started to interview politicians for *Hot Press* some two years previously, while still in Castlerea. *Hot Press*, up to then, had been exclusively concerned with rock music, but I persuaded the editor, Niall Stokes, that there was a way of presenting politics that would not jar with the magazine's music content. I was influenced to some extent by the political interviews that had been appearing intermittently in the *New Musical Express*, usually with left-wing politicians like Ken Livingstone and Tony Benn. But I also had in mind a series of interviews carried in *The Word*, the magazine of the Divine Word Missionaries, based in Donamon, County Roscommon, during the sixties and early seventies.

In publishing terms, *The Word* was way ahead of

its time; in the context of religious publishing, it was revolutionary. As well as reports from the Divine Word mission outposts, it contained a variety of material of social, political and cultural relevance. My father bought it every month. *The Word* interviews were conducted by a range of journalists, including John Skehan, Desmond Rushe and, on at least one occasion, Geraldine Kennedy, who would later become famous as one of Sean Doherty's phone-tapping victims. More often than not, however, the interviews were conducted by the editor of *The Word*, Brother Paul, who created the format and fashioned the style and tone of the conversations. The interviews were not 'profiles' in the conventional sense: they did not contain any editorial comment from the journalist. They were reports of conversations with their subjects, published in question-and-answer format. There is a belief in some journalistic quarters that this approach to interviewing is simply a cover for laziness, or an attempt to conceal the journalist's inability to write; but nothing can be further from the truth.

The Word interviews provided some of the most intimate and insightful glimpses of many of the leading figures of their day, including Sean Lemass, Liam Cosgrave, Gay Byrne, Conor Cruise O'Brien, Brian Friel, Christy Brown, Kate O'Brien, and innumerable other political, artistic and clerical figures – including frequent interviews with leading Protestant clergymen. The subjects were asked about their views of the major issues of the day and about their personal philosophies and outlooks; but they were also asked about their hobbies, their families, their favourite books, about their holidays, their heroes, and their views of themselves. The interviews were discontinued sometime in the mid-seventies and, a decade later, had not been matched in the Irish print media.

One of the aims of the *Hot Press* interview was to recreate this type of forum to allow well-known cultural and political figures an opportunity to reveal themselves to the public in a manner which, though rigorous and probing, allowed the subjects the maximum control over the presentation of their personalities in print. The arrangement had one additional advantage: because it was almost invariably a question-and-answer format, with usually just a couple of introductory paragraphs by the journalist, public figures who might otherwise have declined to be interviewed proved willing to submit themselves. Charles J. Haughey was the biggest fish so far.

When I met Haughey, I did not like him much. He seemed to have some great need to be superior, to take the upper hand. He reminded me of how certain small people make themselves felt in the presence of those taller than themselves. First they get you to sit down, then they stand up.

Haughey, according to rumour, did this sort of thing all the time. He appeared to want to be feared at least as much as he was loved. His personal machine operated, they said, as a reign of terror. His aides were afraid of their lives of him, and would do almost anything in order to avoid his wrath. 'What part of Dublin did you say you were from?' he asked me. 'Oh, I'm not from Dublin. I'm from Roscommon.' 'Mmmm,' he said. 'Roscommon, mmmmm, Roscommon, mmmmm,' as though this were some kind of profound comment, as though he knew a lot of people who came from Roscommon and did not think much of them.

I was nervous and mumbled. Sometimes, in asking a question, I would gloss over something of which I was less than certain, just to move things along and get him spouting once more. He would listen carefully to what I had said, pick it apart and place it back in front of me. 'Sure you don't know what the fuck you're talking about at all.' When this happened, I would sit there silently, thinking of him eating the steak that had been rubbed all over the chef's private parts, and wishing I could have been there.

But he gave me what I discovered afterwards was the goods. It was well known that Haughey was almost incapable of saying two words without one of them being 'fuck' or 'shit' or 'cunt'. In the presence of my tape recorder, he 'fucked' his way through two sides of a sixty-minute tape.

When he was young, he said, if a guard told you to fuck off, you fucked off as quick as you could. He could instance a load of fuckers in the country whose throats he'd cut and shove over the nearest cliff. He spoke of the Irish people and their love of politics; they were fifty times more politically conscious, he said, than 'their bovine British counterparts'. Haughey told me about his childhood, his schooldays, of his secret desire to steal a car and go joyriding, about how sorry he was to have been too old for the sexual revolution of the 1960s. One journalist would note later that, in the course of his *Hot Press* interview, Mr Haughey used one 'Jasus', one 'Jesus Christ', seven 'fuck's and three 'shit's. From time to time as we talked, the Fianna Fáil leader would point to the tape recorder and say, 'Turn off that fuckin' intimidating yoke.' But I would mumble something about my shorthand not being up to scratch and we would press on.

Within a week all this would be taking up acres of space in the newspapers. I found it strange that, although reporters shied away from reporting the way Haughey really spoke in private, they seemed to have no problem running extracts from the *Hot Press* interview in the newspapers, leavened with a sprinkling of righteous indignation about the fact that one of their codes had been breached.

People asked afterwards if Haughey had appeared drunk while I was talking to him, but the explanation was much less interesting than that. I had gone along expecting to be given an interview full of the usual platitudes of politicians. In retrospect, I realised that Haughey was clearly confused about the precise status of our conversation – whether we were speaking for direct quotation, or to allow me to fill in some background in my descriptions of his epic struggle to fulfil his destiny. As the interview progressed, it occurred to me that he was being a little more direct than I had expected; but because such conversations seldom suggest the effect they will take on in print, I thought nothing of it. I did think it strange, however, when he said as I was leaving that I should call him the following week 'for some direct quotes'; but since this was likely to mean a tapeful of banalities, I decided to go home and leave the phone off the hook.

When I read over the transcript of the interview, it seemed to me that its implications were far greater than if I had written an article tabulating the details of Haughey's personal finances and proving that he had accumulated his wealth by dubious means. Somewhere in here was a little of the mystery of Charles Haughey, the way he courted dislike, the way he diced with political mortality.

His *Hot Press* interview may have had a large or a

small effect on the subsequent rehabilitation of Charles Haughey. At the time it was published, in December 1984, he was out of office, skulking disconsolately in the Dáil chamber, the unhappy and hapless leader of the opposition. He had been banished there in a wave of media outrage following the outlandish episodes of the GUBU period. Just over two years later he would be back in government with the selfsame media behind him. Analysing this transformation, Joe Joyce, a journalist who had written a book about the excesses of the GUBU period, wrote about the interview in an article called 'The Beatification of Charles J. Haughey' for *In Dublin* magazine: '[Haughey's] *Hot Press* interview', wrote Joyce, 'had him talking in public with uncharacteristic bluntness, but showed him to be a more sympathetic and interesting person than the phoniness of his formal interviews. His initial horror that his interviewer had not cleaned up his language in print – as journalists frequently do – subsided when the overall reaction was positive.'

In such ways do people who lead people make themselves up: with a little help from ambivalent bystanders. In Ireland, up to the time of Sean Lemass, politicians emerged, in much the same way as monarchs in other countries, from the mists of history. Both de Valera and Lemass were military men turned politicians: they belonged to a process that had its roots in the past. Perhaps at some level, conscious or otherwise, Charles Haughey had sensed that the ground in which these roots had thrived had become fallow from over-use. He would have to plant his legend somewhere, though in a way that would allow it to be fertilised by the legends that had preceded it.

Haughey was perhaps the first post-independence Irish

politician who would be totally the product of his own and his country's imagination. He knew, too, that this imagination had been cast in the mould of division and mutual suspicion. Eamon de Valera had continued to capture that imagination to his dying day and beyond, precisely because those who did not love him hated him with a vengeance. If they had stopped hating him, those who loved him would cease to care. He would have withered on the vine of national indifference.

Haughey lived his life at the mercy of the public imagination, and yet he kept a tight rein on its ambiguities and contradictions. His personality was constantly in flux, reinventing itself in response to what he detected in the public mood. Often he would make what others perceived as U-turns, because not to do so would mean the end of his political ambitions. To his admirers he was a realist, a pragmatist and a believer in the art of the possible. To his detractors he was an opportunist, a chameleon and a fake.

Haughey seemed to have conducted a detailed study of the dynamics of power, as a mechanic would study the workings of a new type of carburettor. He had calculated all the apparent contradictions that were the fuel of politics – the way, for instance, that people like their leaders to be of them and yet, at the same time, above them. He possessed an acute understanding of the necessary schizophrenia of politics: the need to have a number of different personae – some for commanding respect, others for cultivating popularity.

He was the fat chieftain. He had bought himself a Georgian mansion on the outskirts of Dublin – a fact that was common knowledge, and yet he was sparing about the amount of exposure he allowed to be given to the house. Once in a while he would agree to be photographed standing outside its impressive doorway, but this was usually for consumption abroad, for the bovine readers of the British Sunday glossies to fulminate over. On one occasion I asked him to allow us to photograph him at the front of the house, for *In Dublin*. He declined. 'Too much Georgian splendour,' he explained.

It was as though Haughey had calculated carefully the effect of each and every move he might make, each pose he might strike, and weighed up its advantage or disadvantage on the balance of possibilities. Even in the company of much taller men (he himself is a little over five feet) he managed to stand out by dint of his stiff, erect gait. His legs and arms were the only parts of his body which moved, and they did so with a slow, slightly exaggerated rhythm. In public he maintained a grave, statesmanlike expression. He had cultivated a repertoire of gestures and mannerisms, culled from a wide range of world leaders past and present, which allowed him to assume a monarchical demeanour, and communicate across great distances with people he had taught to understand this semaphoric language. When he met Fianna Fáil activists from some far-flung part of the country, they would expect him to know who they were. Approaching such people, perhaps at the Fianna Fáil Ard Fheis, he would in an instant dispel any doubts about how he regarded them by a simple upward sweep of both hands. These little indulgences served to infuriate further those who thought him pompous and insufferable, so the fires of love and hate were fanned with equal and escalating ferocity.

The relationship between Haughey and the Irish people, it seemed to me, had been brought by mutual conspiracy to the pitch of a strange and epic love affair, with Haughey as a Heathcliff figure. I wrote this once in an article: 'Back in the sixties it was love at first sight between the Irish nation and the brave young suitor who vowed vengeance against the wicked stepmother who had mistreated his love for several centuries. The stepmother, however, conspired with some of the more wimpish suitors to banish our hero from the presence of the one he loved. We settled, for a while, for second best, though the flames of love continued to flicker deep down.'

I was ambiguously in favour of Haughey. He made a certain kind of confused sense of the bewilderment I felt about politics. During the 1987 general election campaign, I wrote in *In Dublin* that because politics was about much more than power, because it was also about a country's sense of self, we should vote for Fianna Fáil. Since we thought of ourselves as an interesting and enigmatic people, we could hardly escape from someone who had designed himself in precisely that image.

Colm Tóibín called me up and laughed loudly down the phone, repeating again and again the last line of my article: 'Let us embrace our destiny.' Charles Haughey might have written it himself.

15

The Man Who Shouted Stop

Towards the end of Fianna Fáil's brief tenure of office in 1982, when Charles Haughey was under attack from Dublin 4 elements that had crept into his own party, he went on radio one Sunday lunchtime and told the media and his detractors that they should 'go dance on somebody else's grave'. He was going nowhere in a box for the moment. Even some of his closest allies felt that this optimism was misplaced. The *Irish Press*, the paper founded by de Valera himself, had published a political obituary of Haughey. The journalists who had made a living out of hating him for so long were strangely jubilant, as though it had not occurred to them that with Haughey gone they would have nobody to attack. But Haughey seemed to be in more trouble than he appeared to be able to grasp. He was due to face a vote of confidence by his own parliamentary party, and even some of his own front bench were beating a crocodile-tear-stained path to his door to advise him that the time had come to step down.

The next morning, in the *Irish Times*, John Healy wrote a column about an entirely different matter. It was about

Garret the Good, and gave no hint of what had been happening to the man whom Healy had christened The Golden Boy. At the end of the column, disconnected from the main piece, was a short paragraph requesting that anyone who had a vacancy for a bunch of coffin dancers should speak now or forever hold their peace. Healy was saying something that had now reached the point of being ludicrous: that Charles Haughey would survive the latest heave against his leadership. The editor of the *Irish Times*, Douglas Gageby, was dubious about this. He himself had long been an admirer of Haughey, and Healy was his best friend, but even he had to admit that, this time, Healy was sticking his neck out too far. He rang Healy and asked him if he really wanted the paragraph to stand. 'Leave it,' Healy grunted, 'gloriously right or gloriously wrong.'

I cannot pin down the time when I first became aware of John Healy, but I do know that it was probably much later than most of the people I would meet in Dublin who seemed to resent him so much. Our family, like Healy's, had what he called 'Blueshirt leanings', and so read the *Irish Independent*. The *Irish Press*, of course, was for Fianna Fáilers; the *Irish Times* we considered in some vague way, to be a 'Protestant paper'. I can remember many sunny summer mornings helping my father to make the drops of daily papers in Castlerea, Ballaghaderreen, Frenchpark and Elphin. At each shop you would take a large bale of *Independent*s in one hand and a bale of *Irish Press*es in the other, and struggle towards the doorway. You could carry the bundle of *Irish Times*es in your mouth.

My father was aware of Healy. Sometimes he would buy the *Western People*, in which Healy wrote a column, or take home a stray copy of the *Irish Times*. He would read Healy's column, then leave down the paper and look around, bursting to find someone to make a speech to. If you caught his eye, he would lift the paper again and proclaim: 'He's a great writer, that Healy.' He recognised in Healy's writing the essence of his own experience and view of the world.

But it is one of the contradictions of modern Ireland that many of the people for whom John Healy spoke, the 'great but anonymous' people whose champion he was, were among the last to discover him. We in the West of Ireland were aware of his presence, sure – how could you not be? He was Our Man in the *Times*. But most of us read him considerably less regularly than those to whom he pleaded our case. Some of us, of course, neglected to read him for other reasons: because he told the truth and we could not bear it.

After I had returned home to take over the mailcar run, I began reading the *Irish Times* every day. Whenever I had a few minutes to kill along the road in the mornings, I would prise a copy from one of the Elphin bundles, open it carefully at the page I wanted and, after reading, would roll it up again and put it back in the bale. On Mondays and Saturdays, the first thing I read was Healy's 'Sounding Off' column. I did not read it particularly for what Healy said about the issue with which he was dealing on any given day. I read it for the way he wrote and the view of the world he articulated. Healy, I knew in a vague sort of way, in his day had been the best journalist in the country: his writings about politics had given him a stature which overshadowed all others. Now, he was coasting. His 'Sounding Off' column was often repetitive and lopsided, sometimes cranky, but was always colourful and occasionally brilliant. That was the sort of journalist he was.

I could not but wonder at the neck of him; he seemed to thrive on annoying those who found him hard to take. He called himself 'Healy' and wrote of himself as though he were someone else – someone he admired and indulged but knew he also had to defend: a sort of precocious younger brother who was always getting into scrapes with the boys from the posh end of town. 'I am prepared to let events proceed, as is my wont, and allow time to vindicate me as perfectly as it always does', he wrote on one occasion when his latest pronouncement looked as if it were coming unstuck. 'Some love me, some hate me, but they all read Healy first.'

He loved to make prophecies about the outcome of elections and other political events. His speciality was writing 'post mortems' for publication *before* polling day. He seemed to get it nearly right most of the time, and spot-on often enough for these pre-election 'inquests' to become legendary. 'I am sure', he would write afterwards, 'that you will pardon my moment of triumph.'

Healy seemed seldom to leave the house except for occasional trips to his native Mayo. He would sit in his front room in Rathmines, or potter around in his greenhouse, listening to the radio, or talking on the telephone to one of a handful of 'sounding posts' – well-placed sources in various parts of the country. 'There's a lot to be said for keeping an eye on things from the old greenhouse. All you need is the old tranny and a sharp ear for the nuance. The last place in the world to read an election is from Kildare Street, where all the noises come at you unfiltered.'

It was Dublin 4 that made me interested in Healy. He had resurrected the phrase, along with another, the 'Donnybrook Set', and had given it a new currency. I realised that he was expressing something, representing something, with which I identified too. Healy and I had a lot in common: we had both been born in the West of Ireland; we were both 'townies', but with roots in the countryside; we had both taken to journalism as a vocation rather than as a career.

I read Healy's books, *Nineteen Acres* and *The Death of an Irish Town*. The first was the story of Healy's mother's family and their smallholding in County Mayo. But it was more than a mere chronicle: it was a great roar of a book, a scream that had an echo in my own life. In *Nineteen Acres* Healy told of his own roundabout journey in search of his roots. It was a story of Irish life in microcosm, and so was more personal than our notions of history could suggest. It told of the O'Donnell family, warts and all, and of their struggle to maintain their smallholding through a civil war, two world wars, an economic depression and the elements, only to come face to face in the seventies with what Healy called the Eurocrats, 'who would dismiss such holdings as rural slums and bulldoze them into bigger, more economic units'. *Nineteen Acres* laid bare the whole of Healy's own life and that of his family. It was a story so true and so real that parts of it, no matter how many times I read them afterwards, always made me cry. Healy had made up his mind, a long time ago, about where he stood on the main issues. He described in detail a trip he had made to America in his twenties, which had taken him into the New World and the future, but just as surely into the past. It had highlighted his awareness of the old ways of doing things, which up until then had lain dormant at the back of his mind. He became, in his own phrase, an apostle for Ireland. He was popularly perceived as a conservative, but in fact he was a radical who espoused an ideology that was anti-ideological long before that term, with the 1989 revolutions in Eastern Europe, became a fashionable one.

Healy's only ideology was the anti-ideology of the land, of the tribe, of the clan. He believed passionately in its doctrine of sharing – the *meitheal*: the clan culture of mutual help and compassion – and its tenets governed every word he wrote or uttered. In *The Death of an Irish Town* he heralded its demise in Mayo, and in *The Land of Us*, a series of articles he wrote for the *Irish Times* in 1985, he celebrated its ascendancy in Japan. *The Death of an Irish Town* was a paperback edition of a series of articles he had written for the *Irish Times* in the late sixties, under the title 'No-one Shouted Stop', about the decline of his home town, Charlestown, County Mayo. The tale of marginalisation and neglect it told could have been about any of a hundred Irish towns, including my own.

I decided to make Healy's acquaintance. Before Christmas 1985, I rang him up and said I wanted to do a profile of him for *In Dublin*. 'Come out to the house,' he said. When I met him, I was struck again by the way the topography of his life seemed to parallel my own. In some way he reminded me of my father. Writing about him was a revelation; the words flowed more easily than they had ever done before. There was a truth about his life which seemed also to contain the truth of my own. I had no need to invent a persona to write about Healy.

Healy, I wrote,

is as much an O'Donnell – his mother's people – as he is a Healy, and he has the signs of both families on him. John's uncle Jim used to say that it was in the nature of the O'Donnells to be stout, and stout Healy certainly is. And his mother used to say of his father's people that all they were good for was 'skitin' round the place . . . They'd let the nettles grow up their backsides so long as there was a dance somewhere they could be off to,' she would say. And when you meet John Healy, feel the warm, firm grip of his spade-like hand, sense that instant at-ease feeling he puts out, have the radio turned down for you and are put at the receiving end of his leisurely and gruff wisdom, you know that John Healy is also as much a Healy as he is an O'Donnell. It isn't all that difficult to imagine that, if things had been just a little bit different, this man who is on top of the journalistic heap, sitting here in the neat, cosy front room of his Rathmines home, drinking brandy and wine and tea as the humour takes him, could with a different throw of the dice be sitting in a small slated house in Mayo with a piece of twine around his coat and the nettles coming up to the back door. And you know, too, that even if the tools and accoutrements are different – a radio in the corner instead of a graip, a typewriter in the next room rather than a scythe – it's still the same Healy that you're getting for your money.

Healy liked the profile. He rang me up when it came out: 'You got me there, oul shtock.' From then on he wrote for *In Dublin*, and later for *Magill*. I was about the same age as his two sons, both of whom had emigrated to Australia; the ironies of this were not lost on either of us.

I began to learn why Healy had become such a defender of Charles Haughey. He told me of when Haughey had become Minister for Agriculture in the mid-sixties and had asked Healy to take him down to the West of Ireland to see how farming there was fixed: 'We'll walk this bloody snipegrass you're always on about, Healy.' They spent a day driving through the villages and townlands of Roscommon and Mayo. They visited farms and sat drinking tea by the fire while people told of what they needed to make their lives better. On the way back, Healy showed Haughey the O'Donnell family farm near Carracastle. That trip, as far as I could make out, had been enough to make Healy decide to champion Haughey's cause. Haughey had listened, with genuine interest rather than mere politeness, and he had gone back to Dublin and done something about it, introducing the 'farmers' dole', which Healy said should more correctly have been called a subsidy to live on the land. 'I think,' he told me, 'that Charles Haughey has the same hunger that Lemass had, except that he has refined it more.' This belief was unshakable: Haughey had shown him long ago whose side he was on. He was on our side, Healy believed, and it behoved us to return the favour.

When Healy died, on Little Christmas Day (6 January) 1991, the many tributes to his memory placed great emphasis on his contribution to Irish journalism. All were agreed that, despite what were perceived as his many failings, his early *Irish Times* column, 'Backbencher', had changed the face of Irish political reporting. This was all true, but it was not even half the true meaning of Healy.

To sum him up like that would be to place journalism in a vacuum, to confine Healy's legacy to the role of commentator, a hurler on the ditch. He was, in fact, as we all should aim to be, an organic part of his own life and times.

It has often been said in criticism of Healy that he really only ever wrote about himself, that other people, whether they were statesmen or smallholders, had little more than walk-on parts. When I became editor of *Magill*, I asked Healy to write a profile of his old friend Donogh O'Malley, the charismatic and revolutionary Minister for Education who had introduced free education in the sixties. Healy wrote an impassioned and colourful piece which, like an earlier article I had asked him to write about Charles Haughey for *In Dublin*, conspired to consume half the pages of the magazine. Vincent Browne was not happy about this. 'You're taking too much notice of that fellow Healy,' he said. 'Healy thinks he's a guru. He wants to write himself into history.'

This was true. Healy did not see himself as belonging on the sidelines. Immersed in the mystery of his own life and times, he had fashioned a vision of what he wanted his country to become. Behind the deliberately glib arrogance of 'Backbencher', there beat a heart full of passion and idealism. His vision was a wholly integrated one. After a period of disillusionment, during which he had made an attempt to emigrate to America, Healy had come to a decision that he would not just make the best of his country but would make his country The Best. Being The Best was everything: 'Second-best is for the rest.'

He set about this purpose with determination and deviousness, actively courting leading politicians, most of whom, given the nature of Irish politics, were visionless by definition. He bent their ears and made his visions theirs. His fondness for Haughey led Healy to become relatively marginalised in the latter years of his life. He had defended The Great National Bastard, and that was unforgivable. Even his friends became tired of his endless defence of what to many of them had become indefensible. You could not get people who denigrated Healy to accept that Healy was not, at any time, a Fianna Fáiler by inclination. He had no time for de Valera, for example, and in the general election of 1973 had declared for the coalition. Since then he had backed Haughey. He did so, first of all, because he believed that Haughey was the best chance the country had. But he also backed Haughey, and continued to back him, because if the Dublin 4 pack was against him, then, very well, Healy would be on his side to even the score. But he had an eye, too, for Haughey's flaws. 'Once in the sixties', he wrote in *In Dublin*, 'Douglas Gageby asked me what I thought of the idea of Haughey as Taoiseach and I said: "On the condition that I could police his government twenty-four hours out of twenty-four, to protect him from his friends".'

'I won't be put in eggboxes,' he would say. Nor could he. Just when you thought you had the measure of him, he would do or say something to take you completely by surprise. He confounded those who had labelled him a 'conservative' by taking the 'liberal' side in the referendums of 1983 and 1986. 'Backbencher' had been his Cryptic Jim. Its style was arrogant and loud: 'Don't mess with me, sham.' It is how Healy will be remembered, although he himself was not at all like that. Yet his real and invented personae had things in common. In both guises he loathed

Dublin 4 and its lack of truth, its attempts to deny the reality of Irish life, its failure to understand that politics was, first of all, about people. You could not impose systems or ideologies on those who had no use for them. Left and right was the way you learned to goose-step, but it had nothing to do with Irish politics. 'We are a peasant people,' he would say. 'We are just now beginning to learn about democracy.'

He gave me a new map of Dublin:

The city is only a string of villages. Irishtown and Ringsend are as much villages as Charlestown. You have to explain more to people in Ireland what the culture of the land is than you have in Japan. *They* know it. But it was never taught to us. We were never told growing up that the people of the land had the first uniculture. It goes from the edge of Achill out to the Steppes of Russia. I can go to any village and I will know the structure immediately. I will know the value system. There'll be small little variations, but basically it'll be the same. And it's not class distinction, as a lot of people think. What they're mistaking is the hierarchical structure – and that's not the same thing.

Contrary to his image as a rural bootboy, a culchie out of his proper milieu, Healy loved the city:

I remember the year Mayo won the All Ireland Championship: 1950. I remember going down along the quays and seeing the September sun warm on the old red bricks and saying: 'This is an old town; this is a great town. This is a town to come into and be the best in.'

Because we were the best that year, in football. I can still remember seeing those warm red bricks and feeling the antiquity of the city. I have as much of a feeling about Dublin as I have about Mayo and the West.

But he was not a citizen of the Universal City. 'People say that the bright lights attract, but that's a fallacy. The bright lights never meant anything to me.'

I had never met a man, apart from my father, who seemed to understand so much. He could tell what would happen in the future of Irish politics because he had understood its past – not just in terms of politics and history, but as experienced in the lives of his fellow Irish people.

Still, I too sometimes wondered about his veneration of Charles Haughey. I had no doubt that Healy passionately believed in Haughey, and that he was galvanised in that belief by the bile of Haughey's opponents. But what of Haughey himself, I wondered. Was he worthy of Healy? Did he deserve the support of such a man?

Once, early in the morning, I had to go out to Haughey's house with a photographer to take his picture for the cover of *In Dublin*. Healy had written an article about Haughey, entitled 'Down to Our Last Hero', a great twenty-thousand-word rationalisation of why we should now, in the dying days of the 1983–87 coalition, give Haughey the last chance he deserved. Healy had told me that Haughey had around his house a number of interesting species of tree, which he had imported and planted himself. In Healy's eyes, these were evidence of Haughey's commitment to the environment. 'Get him photographed standing in front of his trees,' Healy instructed me.

That morning I carefully guided Haughey in the direction of various trees around his house. Click, click. Click, click. After a time he became impatient. 'Have you enough of fuckin' trees now. What the fuck is all this stuff about trees?' I explained that Healy had expressed a wish that Haughey's commitment to nature and the environment be clearly communicated. 'Healy,' he said, 'has fuckin' trees on the brain.' I searched for irony in his eyes, but could detect none. There was something in his tone that made me wince, that seemed almost a betrayal of Healy's loyalty to him. It reminded me, for some reason I could not focus on, of the time I had spoken to Colm Tóibín about Healy and what he believed about us being really, deep down, a peasant people. 'Peasants, John,' he replied, his irony buried deep beneath impatience, 'are stupid people – with thick, white legs.'

16

A Mood Almost Proustian

As far as I could work out, my father's liking for Sean Doherty dated from 1979, the time when Charles Haughey had become leader of Fianna Fáil. Doherty had been one of the infamous Gang of Five who effectively had staged a bloodless coup within Fianna Fáil, forcing the resignation of Babyface Lynch, and ensuring the accession to power of Charles Haughey. Doherty had immediately become a Minister of State in Haughey's new regime.

Like many things in politics, it was the coincidence of these happenings with the death of my father's brother, John, in England, which led to a sympathy for Doherty being perhaps permanently forged in my father's brain. He had not seen his brother for many years, and could not bring himself to travel to England for the funeral; my sister Margaret and I went instead.

Because he had always kept himself to himself, not many people in the town even knew that my father had a brother, much less that he had died. Since John had had no remaining friends alive in Ireland, it was decided not to put a notice in the paper. But in the middle of December, shortly after Haughey's assumption of power, my father was making the evening collection from Elphin post office. He pulled up outside and, being early, sat in the van for a few moments to let time catch him up. A big black car flashed through the Main Street, causing passersby to swivel gawpingly around. When it reached the top of the street, instead of turning left for Carrick-on-Shannon, the car swept majestically around and retraced its tracks to the post office. Sean Doherty stepped out from the front passenger seat, approached my father's van and tapped on the window. The ropes were untied. 'I'm sorry to hear about your trouble, Tom.' Doherty stood on the street and talked to my father for a few minutes before climbing back into his state car and driving off.

From that day onwards, my father would not allow a bad word about Sean Doherty to be said in his presence. Once or twice when he would pay glowing tribute to Doherty's decency, I might try to get him going: 'All those politicians spend their lives writing mass cards and going to funerals.'

'How well he knew about it and nobody else did.'

'He'd know less.'

He did not care. To him the gesture was enough; the motivation was not his concern. 'No matter what you stand for, or what you believe in, if you don't treat people properly it's no use.' He was not humourless about it: when I told him the story of Doherty pulling a fast one on Terry Leyden over a funeral, he was still laughing days afterwards at the good of it. But the personal touch, no matter how devious the mechanism, was to him beyond price. Even if politicians had to work hard at being human, was this not better than the alternative? 'Humanity,' he would say, 'is the white heat of politics. If you haven't got that, you have nothing.'

In Dublin I found myself drawn to Doherty, just as I was drawn to Healy. There was no escaping it. Once someone had picked up on your accent and discovered that you were from Roscommon, the conversation almost invariably followed a similar pattern. 'Aha, Doherty country!' It was said always with a mixture of disapproval and knowing glee.

'That's right, yeah.' Your reply would always be non-committal. It was one thing to disapprove of Doherty among his own people, but quite another to join in an outsider's prejudice about him.

'He's some boyo!'

'So they say.'

Doherty's name had become a byword for a very specific condition in Irish politics. The media line was that his was the politics of the stroke, the fix, the parish pump, of graft, crookery and whatever you're having yourself; he was the archetypal rural redneck, corrupted by power. The legends of his infamy had long since blurred and merged, so that truth and legend had become as one. He was the man, they said, who had tried to have a Garda sergeant disciplined for doing his duty; he had been involved in a late-night car crash in Kerry in the company of a blonde pop singer to whom he was not related; he had tapped the telephones of two of the country's leading journalists, and had involved the most senior officers in the country's police force in the bugging of a conversation between party colleagues.

As a result of the public outrage at some or all of these real or apocryphal occurrences, Doherty had been expelled temporarily from the Fianna Fáil parliamentary party. He said at the time that he had gone along quietly with the decision in order to save his party leader from having to spill his own blood. Doherty was Haughey's sacrificial lamb to atone for the sins of the GUBU days.

In Roscommon, people rallied to Doherty. In their minds the picture was just as blurred, but the predominant image was of someone, one of them, who was on their side, who was under attack from without. Few would hear a bad word against him. Even those who were opposed to him for party political reasons jumped to his defence at the merest hint of censure by outsiders. The clans closed in around him.

I went back to Castlerea about once every three weeks. Going home was difficult, and coming back to Dublin equally so. It had nothing to do with the state of the roads. Approaching Castlerea gave me a surging feeling in the pit of my stomach, as though I had just gone over a sudden and interminable hump in the road. Like an astronaut re-entering the earth's atmosphere, I could almost feel the resistance tugging at the sides of the car. The resistance really was inside myself, as though the distance I was travelling was through the cells and tissues of my own brain.

When I went to Castlerea, it took me two whole days to acclimatise, and by then it was time to start back. Then in Dublin, I would sink into a deep depression which might last for days. I talked about it to Healy. He said he felt something like this when he went to his house in Achill: the first couple of days he would spend in a deep, depressed sleep. The cliché had it that the 'pace of life' was different, but such a phrase only mocks the meaning of what I am talking about.

There was plenty of cause for depression. The town was changing out of all recognition. The changes were difficult to pin down, though they had their more obvious, physical manifestations. There were the inevitable fast-food take-aways which had begun to infect many such towns in the West and Midlands. On Main Street, in the shop where old Lizzie Gallagher had once sold her Hospital Sweepstake tickets, there was such a joint called American Stars. Gone were most of the old family-run shops, like Miss Kelly's, where once, if you had five minutes to wait, you would get the nicest ice-cream cone on earth. Now there were video games, slot machines and throbbing music to urge you up and on. I could see all around me the evidence of the eighties catchpenny culture: the shops and pubs with every kind of gimmick and racket to bring in a few bob, the everyday urban images of urgent, relentless consumption.

To walk around was to be a stranger in a strange place, and yet to have the ghostly presence of your former self hovering tantalisingly out of your field of vision. For all the evidence of consumerism, there was a diminishing pool of consumers from whose reluctant fists the cash might be prised. Saturday in many shops was like a Monday – the traditional closed day – ten years before. Shopkeepers stood in their doorways, hoping to lure in the odd passerby. They all had the same story: trade was 'middling' at best. Dyar's bakery on Main Street, which had hummed for decades with the shouts and activity of work, was closed and derelict. John Hunt's record shop had ceased to sell records: all its customers had left town. Even the railway station was no longer a railway station; in the internal and mysterious language of CIE, it had been reduced to the status of a 'Halt'.

Castlerea had been a market town, but now the Market Square served as a car park, on which, the odd Friday or Saturday, a van might stop and have its back doors opened to reveal a few tattered bundles of cabbage plants. There were still a couple of factories in the demesne, but they employed only handfuls of people in highly specialised work. The only serious employer in the town was the psychiatric hospital, and even this seemed to be on borrowed time. Government cutbacks had put the writing on the wall.

People were bemused and baffled by what had happened to them. They seemed to accept, as a matter of course, that their children were growing up merely to go away; and yet, because of the sheer everydayness of this, the anger it caused could not be expressed in a direct manner. Among those still in the town were some of my former classmates, a number of whom had jobs, though many had not. Those who had were working hard, usually in the trade or business their fathers had built and handed on; those who had no work skulked and brooded in pubs all day long, playing darts or pool, sipping pints with excruciating slowness and shouting abuse at one another across the counter.

'You're some cunt.'

'Geddup, ya bollix.'

'You have your shite.'

'Kiss my arse, yacuntya.'

This was their way of keeping reality at bay, of relating to one another without having to discuss how they really felt about what had happened to them. The language of jibes, cheerful obscenities and snorts of derision allowed them to live with themselves and each other by removing from conversation all prospect of seriousness.

This was a place in which my generation had been reared in the vague but tangible optimism of the rising tide that would raise all boats. We had stood and gawped at the Man in the Mohair Suit. We had carried lighted torches for our own cabinet minister. We had been led to believe that we would inherit the earth.

To incur the wrath of the people you had left behind, it was not necessary to have done anything to worsen their plight, but simply to have escaped a similar devastation yourself. 'You're doin' all right for yourself, yacuntya.' You played it down. 'Not too bad; they haven't copped on to me yet.' 'You were only a cunt, the best day ever you were.'

And yet, through all this, they remained steadfastly loyal to their town. Within the community, they might acknowledge that the place was 'going down the tubes', but in the presence of outsiders they would neither raise nor tolerate such negativity. Their loyalty was confused and contradictory, but it was also fierce and vengeful.

A woman journalist came once from Dublin to write a story about the town for one of the big American papers, the *New York Times* or the *Washington Post*. She had been commissioned to find an Irish town that was suffering from the typical effects of unemployment and emigration. She had asked around in political circles and had been told by a couple of the area's local representatives that she could not hope to find a worse spot than Castlerea. The journalist arrived in town and began interviewing the shopkeepers and community busybodies. The weekend after her departure, I met a friend in Mulvihill's, who told me that at long last someone was going to have to take notice of the way things had gone in the town. The *Washington Post*, no less, – or was it the *New York*

Times? – was going to carry a big write-up on the local unemployment and emigration levels and the effects they were having on the community. I asked him whom she had spoken to and he reeled off a few names. I expressed surprise that the individuals in question had been as frank as he was leading me to believe. 'We have nothing to lose,' he said.

A month or so later, a summary of the finished article appeared in the *Roscommon Herald*. Castlerea was described as a 'black spot', a wasteland, and by a number of other phrases which, if anything, underestimated the situation. The town went mad. The matter was raised at meetings of everything from the Chamber of Commerce to the County Council. Who had spoken to this woman? Who had put her up to this? How could they expect industrialists to come over from America after a picture like that had been painted in the most distinguished newspaper in the United States? The most vocal critics of all were people who I knew had given interviews to the journalist, in which they had said what a terrible kip the town had become. They decided to blame me: since I was the only one from town who was known in journalistic circles in Dublin, I must have put the journalist up to it. Even the people she had interviewed managed to persuade themselves of this, and would shoot me dark looks in the street.

A lot of people were listening a great deal less to much of the programming coming at them over the national airwaves. I was not surprised. To listen to RTE radio on the second or third day of a visit back home, when you had become acclimatised, was to have your sense of isolation and alienation heightened to a level that was almost surreal. Pundits discussed the economy, how we had all been 'living beyond our means' and would have to tighten our hairshirts. The people in the hundreds of Castlereas all over the country scratched their heads and tried to remember how they had missed this time of plenty and profligacy.

The people of Roscommon had begun to listen to their own station. Mid-West Radio had been started by a local man, Paul Claffey. Nearly a decade before, I had left CIE to work in the station in its previous incarnation. At that time we were unable to break the stranglehold of the Gay Byrnes and Mike Murphys on the ears of the local population. Claffey had begun as a disc jockey in the swinging sixties, while not yet into his teens; he had played records at the local hops and had done relief for the bands in the Casino. To those of us who were younger, he had been both a role model and a star. Later he had moved into band management and promotions, but was badly burned when the bottom fell out of the showband market. He lost all but one of a string of ballrooms in the West, as well as his pub in Ballinlough, near the Mayo/Roscommon border. Down to his last shilling, Claffey had resurrected Mid-West Radio in Ballyhaunis, broadcasting from a small room at the back of his one surviving hall, the Midas Club. By a curious irony, the factor of emigration, which had destroyed the ballroom business, served now to come to his aid. Claffey had always been, like most of us townies, a rock fan. His own musical preferences had been bands like Horslips and Thin Lizzy. He had once managed The Freshmen, who under his guidance had had a record nominated 'Single of the Week' in Britain's *New Musical Express*.

But the secret of his success, Claffey always claimed, was that, once he got up on a stage, or in behind a microphone, he played whatever the punters wanted to hear. This experience provided him with a set of antennae which missed no nuance in an audience. He could feel, he said, what an audience, even a radio audience, wanted to hear. His days in the courts sorting out his financial affairs had made him conscious of what it meant to need a lift in your day. When he restarted Mid-West, Claffey located a totally untapped appetite in the people he broadcast to. He had begun broadcasting merely to promote the bands he had lined up for the coming weekend at the Midas Club, but now he found that the possibilities of local radio were bigger than he had previously imagined. People who had become disconnected from what RTE was saying to them began to tune in and speak to each other through the medium of the station. Many of them were older people, whose children had left, and so who found themselves alone all day in an empty house. They called up Claffey on the air and asked him to play their favourite come-all-ye's. Some would sing duets with him across the airwaves. One woman, Kathleen Loftus, from outside Ballyhaunis, had an electric organ in her front room. She would phone in, put the telephone down on the organ, and sing 'Danny Boy', 'Amazing Grace' or 'South of the Border, Down Mexico Way'. Paul Claffey had become a superstar in the cultural desert that was the West of Ireland in the latter part of the eighties.

Mid-West Radio was a pure and spontaneous explosion of a set of cultural values that had all but been wiped out by the optimism of the sixties. Claffey was the ultimate pragmatist, and his radio station, unencumbered by grandiose notions, began to provide the kind of service that he sensed his people wanted. There was no pop music: all the pop fans had left. There was country, country and Irish, traditional, and the mix of all three which, when played by oddly named local outfits, functioned as a sort of surrogate folk music. It was the kind of music which, years before, perched high on our platform shoes and thinking we could see for miles, we had pronounced to be as good as dead and good riddance. It was the maudlin music of a darker past, which those of us who had left had come to associate with resignation and despair. On the back of the radio station's success, the local entertainment scene had begun to pick up again, and the same halls which a decade previously had throbbed to the sound of Horslips or Thin Lizzy, now jived again to local stars like Mick Cuffe, Kevin Prendergast and Mick Flavin.

Every Sunday night, Claffey hosted a live spectacular, based on the television gameshow *The Price is Right*, giving away fridges, television sets and holidays in the sun. He wore a white suit and a bow tie that lit up. There were people on the stage to hold up signs saying 'Applause', just as in the real world of television.

Claffey was the star of the show. He flirted with the women and teased and mocked the men, drawing them out and pulling them into his fantasy. He was their Gay Byrne, Mike Murphy and Gerry Ryan all rolled into one. 'I'm the man of your dreams,' he would tell the women, and they would screech their assent. You could not fail to be impressed by the excitement and mystery of it all. On my weekends at home, I would go to the Midas Club and stand there wondering where it all was coming from. One night a man, who was standing beside me as Claffey performed, leaned over: 'There isn't a woman in the place wouldn't give that fella the ride.'

At home my father would listen to the show on the radio. He had never before been a fan of Paul Claffey, especially since it was he who had lured me away from my lovely job in CIE, but now he would not hear a word said against him. 'He's a great crack, that fellow.' There was something here which we both felt but could not yet quite touch. My father's life had become a metaphor, surrounded by other, smaller metaphors. Since retiring, he had withdrawn into the house. His kingdom had been the country and the open road, and now he was housebound, with one direction home. I took him out now and again to see the farms he had bought, to look at the trees we had planted. He would assume his old assurance, scrutinising each tree for signs of stunted growth or other infirmity. We would drive around the roads of Aughaderry, Moyne, Fairymount, Buckhill, but we knew that eventually we had to go home, and this broke both our hearts. I stopped suggesting that we go for drives.

We spoke in metaphors and symbols, the most potent of which was politics. He followed every detail, every move in the political life of the country. There was nothing that he did not know or have an opinion about. Politics became the language which facilitated communication without our having to speak of the unspeakable. It was a limited medium, but it allowed us to communicate across a divide that was greater, now, than the mere 110 miles to Dublin.

I noticed that my father's fervour for Haughey had cooled. He found him funny now, more than he found him inspirational. In office, Haughey had not fulfilled his promise, and out of office he seemed to have been immobilised by his lack of a vision of anything but the road back to power.

Nor did my father like what had happened to Doherty. Haughey had done the dirty on him, he said. He should have stood by him; if you don't stand by people, how could you ever expect people to stand by you? We did not argue, as we might have done a few years before. Not only was I not inclined to attack Doherty among the strangers who despised him, but I could no longer condemn his politics to one for whom they had come to have a vital significance. Doherty, at least, was one of us. Doherty, with all his contradictions, was a sort of cry for help.

In January 1987 a general election was called for one month later. As polling day approached, I considered whether I would vote. I was registered in Castlerea, preferring to vote for and against those whom I knew something about, rather than transferring to a Dublin constituency where I would be voting with a different part of my head. But polling day was midweek and I was not sure if I could get the time off to make the trip home. A couple of weeks before the election, the *Irish Independent* had published an 'Open Letter to the People of Roscommon', written by Bruce Arnold, one of the two journalists whose telephones had been tapped on Sean Doherty's instructions when he was Minister for Justice. Arnold, who had recently been awarded damages arising out of the case in a High Court action, had been the subject of an enigmatic attack by Doherty in a speech made in Elphin at the outset of the campaign. Doherty, referring to the High Court as 'the hanging court', spoke of the urgent need to bring to justice people who had been guilty of high treason.

Now, in the run-up to polling day, Bruce Arnold was

replying over Doherty's head to the Roscommon electorate. He asked them not to vote for Sean Doherty. He wrote, he declared, 'in a mood almost Proustian'. Recalling himself standing in some of the historic locations of Roscommon – Rockingham, Lough Key, Frenchpark, the grave of Douglas Hyde – he praised the county's scenery and historic importance. He seemed to be saying that Roscommon would be a wonderful place if it weren't for all the mucksavages who lived there. Arnold ended with a short remedial lesson in the workings of democracy: 'You have to do it with conscious forethought. You have to vote for him. That does the trick. If enough of you do it, it will get him back in. So you have been warned on that score.'

I thought of the many people I knew who, for motives that were entirely honourable, had voted for Doherty on so many occasions. I thought of the smug, satisfied 'inhabitants' of Dublin 4, who hectored them on the airwaves for their backwardness. I thought of my father, who had washed more politics out of his socks than Bruce Arnold could learn in a lifetime in the Dáil gallery.

Come polling day, I got in my car and headed for home. As I approached Castlerea there was none of the usual resistance in my head. I called to the house. 'Have you been to vote?' He hadn't. We drove to the polling station in the Casino and I asked him if he had read Bruce Arnold's open letter. 'He's only a bowsie, that fella.' We did not discuss how we would vote: he would argue and debate, but he would never dictate. 'There are people all over the world who'd give all they had to be able to go down to the Casino.' It did not seem so ludicrous now.

My father was weak from lack of exercise, from sitting in the house. He was into his eighties now, and when he was in the open air I could see the change in him. He was thinner, shaky on his feet. I linked him into the polling station, his feet feeling unsteadily for a grip on the polished maple floor.

He was as excited as a child in a toyshop, bursting to be asked what he thought. Mrs Carroll, my friend Dermo's mother, was delighted to see us. She was on duty for Fine Gael, and as far as she was concerned we were all good Blueshirts together. My father and I went to our separate booths, made our marks, and then I linked him out again. We sat in the car for a minute looking at the river. 'I voted for Doherty,' I said after a bit. He nodded. 'I was thinking that from the way you were talking.' There were tears in both our eyes as we drove home for tea. His were tears of triumphant laughter.

17

Possession

It began to dawn on me that not alone had Doherty been the focus of a change in my own view of Irish politics, but that, somehow or other, the internal breakdown in the comprehensibility of Irish politics – the way that one part of the country was no longer able to understand the other and did not want to think about it – had come to invest itself in his political personality.

Doherty had started to play a parody of the role that had been invented for him. On the day after Fianna Fáil had been returned to government in 1987, Doherty, who had been the first TD returned to the twenty-fifth Dáil, walked into the visitors' bar in Leinster House, half an hour after closing and ordered a drink for himself and his several companions.

'I'm sorry, Mr Doherty,' the barman said, 'I'm afraid we're closed.' Sean Doherty fixed him with his blue, ironic gaze. 'In that case, you're sacked,' he said loudly, for the benefit of the entire bar. 'Fianna Fáil is back in power now.' Even some of Doherty's companions began to try to make themselves invisible, shrinking far back into their padded seats.

The image of Doherty as a man who wanted power for power's sake had been one of the most constant in the recent election campaign. Fine Gael and the Progressive Democrats had plugged like mad the notion of the spectre of Sean Doherty stalking the land, shafting his enemies and fixing things on behalf of his friends. Now he seemed to want to live up to his reputation.

Doherty stared at the barman, who stared back, unflinching. Doherty turned slowly around and winked broadly at his companions, who collapsed into relieved laughter. Sean Doherty was fighting his demonic public image by sending it up.

Bruce Arnold, in his open letter to the people of Roscommon, had captured beautifully this image of Doherty as some kind of terrifying lynch-lawman, in whose persona irony was draped upon irony, a double-, treble-, quadruple-decker sandwich of good humour, mockery and implied danger. Whenever he and Doherty would meet, he recalled, Doherty would always make jokes about the telephone-tapping incident: 'It is a form of pantomime, where accusations of high treason and threats of the dungeon are interspersed with moments of uproarious comedy and farce. He and his audience pause for a moment of wild slapstick, but he goes on to pass sentence nonetheless.'

Doherty's 'audience' was the people he represented, for whom he had become the embodiment of how they regarded their altered role in the country's politics. They believed that, at heart, Doherty was a decent enough bloke who liked to make mischievous jokes and had an almost boyish delight in the idea of being let loose with the reins of political power. He was a good public representative, who did well by his constituents. Their faith in him had been vindicated when Charlie Haughey had made him a minister. It was not often the people of Roscommon had a minister to boast about.

Doherty had now become something more: a roar of defiance. The more he became hated and reviled, the more abuse Dublin heaped upon him, the more his constituents would seek to protect him. They enjoyed the way he seemed to discomfit Dublin 4. When Bruce Arnold squealed, they would indeed collapse into uproarious laughter. Sean Doherty was Roscommon's way of punishing the people who wished to exclude, dismiss and patronise it.

But the Doherty I knew was just a metaphor. He was still an image flitting in and out of my life. I knew what I had voted for – or rather what I had voted against – but I did not know the man to whom I had given my vote.

Meeting him proved difficult. The party had been keeping him under wraps since his outburst in Elphin had made him a born-again demon and had nearly lost them the election. He had given up drinking and was not socialising. His public utterances were now confined to earnest statements on local issues, subjects like the environment, the single European market and the tourist industry, for which he had not formerly been noted. It had dawned on Doherty that, if he were ever again to obtain high political office, he would need to prove himself a sober and serious-minded person in the eyes of Dublin and the media. This seemed to me to be an almost impossible task.

I called him up and said I wanted to write about him. He was pleasant but evasive. He did not want to do interviews 'at this particular point in time'. I detected suspicion; I was, after all, a member of 'the media'. I told him that my father and I had voted for him in the general election. He laughed: 'I am always available to meet my constituents.' It took three meetings before his scepticism began to thaw. He had a way of looking at you while you were speaking which suggested that he could read your mind and tell if you really meant what you were saying. 'I know people,' he said with his dark and meaningful mixture of mockery and menace. 'I know them better than they think I know them. Sometimes I get to know them better than they know themselves.'

Even when he loosened up, he spoke on three different levels. The first was the official Doherty line: the sayings of the new, reformed Sean Doherty, the man who was off drink and was all business, who was a member of innumerable political and community action groups. This Sean Doherty spoke seriously and solemnly, a statesman concerned to do the best for his people and his country. This persona was entirely for the consumption of Dublin 4.

The second was the ironic Sean Doherty, who spoke with forked tongue in cheek, who would declare his loyalty to the party and its 'democratically elected leader' and who talked of the need for a united front. As he spoke, he would wink periodically at me, a big broad wink that both drew me in and defied me to find a way of betraying to the audience what he really meant. It was as if he was speaking on a telephone to a third party, someone he was trying to mislead, and smirking and winking at me to indicate that he did not mean a word of what he was saying. I asked him if he felt he should have been put back in the cabinet. Oh no, he replied. How could he expect to be in the cabinet with so much other talent available to the Taoiseach? He mentioned the name of a cabinet minister: 'A fine mind!' He named another: 'A brilliant thinker.' He winked again. 'I wouldn't even dream of including myself in what I would describe as that pool of talent!'

It was as though Doherty himself was no longer sure what role he was supposed to be playing, where his true political persona lay. For the political establishment, the party hierarchy, the media, and the people he met in Dublin, he had invented one persona. For the people of Roscommon he was someone different. He had become expert at mixing the two personalities, in varying amounts, depending on the company. But sometimes you got the feeling that the real Sean Doherty was caught between two equally fictitious creations. There were too many different scriptwriters, too many contradictory lines, and irony was not always a great traveller.

A third persona, which as far as I could tell was the real Sean Doherty, emerged only with a growing trust. When certain that he could reveal things that would not be used against him, he would speak of his real feelings: his sense of confusion, his hurt and the grief his family had suffered in his disgrace. 'Take a person – any person – for a week and hammer them. Do it for a month, two months, spend a couple of years at it . . .' He struggled with words to play down his sense of hurt. 'Not very pleasant. I never had a good word printed about me for years. I had the worst possible pictures printed. I can never account for the wild, unbridled madnesses that overcame

206

certain people in journalism at that time. Maybe there was some interplanetary reaction that affected them, or some extraordinary pollution that affected them . . . I don't know.'

His language was not English, but an odd mixture of everyday speech and official jargon. Every phrase was exaggeratedly formal. He would not say 'I haven't got time', but 'I am currently prevented by constraints of time from pursuing that particular course of action.' Sometimes he mixed words up, using them in the wrong places and contexts, in a manner that approached poetry: 'I don't respond to influences or breezes on a willy-nilly, fire brigade basis.' He spoke like this all the time, I noticed, even when he was addressing members of his own family: 'Yes, I have taken full cognisance of the reality that the shops will be closing in half an hour.'

Doherty spoke of politics as though it were a disease. He parodied himself in his political persona, walking around with his hand stuck out in front of him, begging for votes – 'a political spastic'. He fantasised about hiring someone to walk in front of him in Dublin, ringing a bell and shouting 'Unclean! Unclean!' He referred to someone called 'Sean Doherty', as though this person was only loosely connected with himself. 'Sean Doherty has appeared in Knock more often than the Virgin Mary!'

But his underlying intent was clearly serious. This had kept him going, he said, when others might have given up. Politics was not simply a function you performed, like a job or a career, 'it is a condition that permeates one'. He spoke of politics and religion in similar words and phrases. People 'believed' in politics, they 'supported' the Catholic Church. He saw himself in the role of a secular priest, responding to the needs of the people who elected him. He seemed to regard the role of the politician as providing a buffer between the citizen and the fundamentally un-democratic nature of the society to which he ministered:

> In modern society the politician may be the only person left to whom you can talk. There are very few human problems that I haven't been confronted with in my time. And, while you might not always be able to do much, I find that just talking to people and explaining to them, the therapy of that, is important. You come down to very strong human factors, where often emotions, and understanding, and appreciation of people, may have to be called upon. And you realise that what often appears to be the glibness of politics, and the detachment of the politician, must all be set aside. It's a dangerous road to take when you remove the sensibility which the politician must have about what he is doing, and what he represents.

What he was saying was, as my father had told me long before, that humanity was the white heat of politics. 'It's people we represent – not machinery, not corporations, not institutions.'

Doherty was an archetypal figure in Irish politics in the two decades that were overshadowed by the diminutive figure of Charles Haughey. Doherty had been born to politics, the son and grandson of politicians. His father had been a Fianna Fáil county councillor in Roscommon for over twenty years; before that, his maternal grandfather had been a Fine Gael councillor. 'There was a confluence,' he said, 'which resulted in me.' He was steeped in the culture of politics at the point of contact with the voter. In another place, another political era, he might have put in an undistinguished, though honourable, career as a public representative. In the crucible of 1980s Irish politics he had been turned into a symbol in the war between two Irelands. Like John Healy but in a different way, Doherty had become a lightning conductor for the forks of suspicion that darted from one part of Ireland towards another. Throughout the seventies and early eighties, one side – the denizens of Dublin 4 – had invested all their impatience, their embarrassment, their righteous resentment, in the figure of Charles Haughey. Now, in the late eighties, nearly twenty years after the Arms Crisis, they found that Haughey was the only one willing and able to do their dirty work, to knock the national economy back into shape after the failure of their hero, Garret FitzGerald. They needed Haughey for the moment, and Haughey could not achieve power without their support.

But they needed also the lightning conductor, which Doherty provided, to take their feelings of impatience, embarrassment and resentment back safely to earth, to allow them to rationalise what they could never openly admit. And so Haughey strode in the light, while Doherty brooded under the shadow of the flawed pedigree cloud. The newspaper leader-writers, who in the past had lacerated Haughey as a man unfit for public office, now saluted him as the head of 'the best government in the history of the state'. Meanwhile, Doherty and the kind of politics he represented were denigrated and debased. It was not enough to record that Doherty had made mistakes, that he had been overzealous in his loyalty to both his leader and his people, that he was the kind of political cat from whose claws the cream of power might have been more prudently protected. All that he stood for, and all who stood by him, had to be stamped out. He was someone who 'represented all that is worst in Irish politics'. Those who voted for him were a disgrace to their country. A whole way of life had become encased within his personality, and – along with that personality – had been cast out by one side and stubbornly clung to by another. Doherty's native cunning, though awesome in the close quarters of his own territory, did not travel well. He had misunderstood what had happened to him in the past; he had failed to appreciate the sea change that had occurred since the time when, as a member of the Gang of Five, he had campaigned for the elevation of Charles Haughey to the leadership of Fianna Fáil.

Since the hair-raising days of GUBU, Haughey had had to come to terms with the reality of the new ascendancy, with whom any would-be leader of the Irish people must henceforth deal. Doherty had thought his political banishment a temporary matter, a gesture of good faith, an act of purgation. In reality it was a down-payment on Haughey's own future, a future from which Sean Doherty had been permanently banished. Doherty was an extension in so many minds of the demonic characteristics of Charles Haughey, and in the minds of so many others of their resentment of the identification of those characteristics with themselves. The people who had stood by Doherty through thick and thin had been making a far more complex and fundamental statement than either Haughey or his erstwhile enemies understood, and they too had been banished for their pains. Next time they would need a different mode of expression to make themselves clear. Doherty's value as political currency was running out. Rehabilitation was a non-runner. He was a politician without the means ever again to assume high office, and as such had been disconnected from the source of his power. He was the victim of a wasting disease that was slowly rendering him politically impotent. Even if Haughey fell under a bus, his demons would continue to reside in the breast of Sean Doherty.

Doherty was a man possessed, a man in dire need of political exorcism. He had been cast out from the temple of political power and would not be readmitted. Short of going back to the beginning, with a new face and identity, there did not seem to be any way in which he could ever again be just an ordinary politician, or that a vote for him could be a simple statement of preference.

18

Acts of Grave Political Cannibalism

Charles Haughey was quoting Shakespeare again:

> O father Abram, what these Christians are,
> Whose own hard dealing teaches them suspect
> The thoughts of others!

It was Saturday 3 June 1989, about halfway through the campaign of the fifth general election within a decade. Before he had called the election, Haughey and his minority Fianna Fáil government had been soaring high in the opinion polls, and had the almost universal support of the press, which previously had calumniated him at every opportunity. Backed by Alan Dukes's Fine Gael in its avowed aim of 'taking the tough decisions on the economy', the government had looked safe for at least another year. But such was the consensus in support of its economic policies, that Haughey had decided to take advantage of his new-found favour by making an unscheduled run to the country in search of the overall majority that so far had eluded him.

The campaign up to that point had been a non-event. The media and main political parties were agreed on the substantive issue of the government's handling of the economy. Essentially Fianna Fáil was implementing the Doheny and Nesbitt agenda, cutting back on public spending, and in particular on health services. The Fianna Fáil election slogan of the previous election, 'Health Cuts Hurt the Sick, the Old and the Handicapped', had become a black national joke. The dean of the DANSE, Colm McCarthy, for the past couple of years had been employed in an advisory capacity by the government, pointing out where public spending cuts might be made. The old hostility between Haughey and the press had gone. Journalists were openly laughing at the jokes with which he nowadays peppered his public addresses, and queuing up afterwards to bask in his munificent attention and approval.

Because of this consensus, the campaign had been dull; the only real issue was the wisdom of holding an election at all. Such was the dearth of ideas that the press conferences of all the political parties had been more or less monopolised by Vincent Browne and his *Sunday Tribune* elite corps, asking the various leaders how their parties were funded and whether or not they themselves had ever profited from their involvement in politics.

That Saturday morning, in the Shelbourne Hotel, Browne had been pressing Haughey on the nature of his relationship with the beef baron, Larry Goodman. At that point, Haughey, drawing himself up to the fullest extent of his stature, had delivered the quotation from *The Merchant of Venice*. It was, he said, 'particularly apposite in the case of Mr Browne'.

About the time this was going on, my father died. He had been in good form up to the night before, and had gone to bed chuckling gleefully after watching an election dogfight on *Today Tonight*. He awoke about ten when my mother brought him up his cup of tea, but lay back and died before he had drunk half of it. I had been due to go home that weekend, but had delayed to cover the morning press conference. I wrote my article about the exchange between Haughey and Browne, delivered it to the *Sunday Independent* office, and went back home to collect some things. Two minutes after I walked in, the phone rang. They had been trying to reach me for the past couple of hours.

The weekend of the funeral is still like a dim daze, and I can recall it only in part. I remember clearly the arrival, on Sunday afternoon, of Sean Doherty in a flurry of cars. He was campaigning in two elections – the general election and the one for the European Parliament, which was to be held on the same day – and would be unable to make the funeral.

He was conscious of the need to underscore the knowingness between us. I had travelled with him on his campaign, and we were both aware of what the funeral drill involved for a politician. You waited until the crowd had gathered before making your entrance. You shook hands solemnly with the bereaved. If none of your political opponents showed up, you clocked up a few points. In Castlebar, a couple of months earlier, we had been to the funeral of a local Fianna Fáil activist. As we climbed back into the car, Doherty had rubbed his hands in glee: 'No sign of Killilea!' (Mark Killilea was his running mate in the Connacht/Ulster constituency. My father, as a young man,

214

had driven Killilea's father, also called Mark, who had been a Galway TD for much of the four decades between the early twenties and his retirement in 1961.)

Communication was difficult in that web of irony and contradiction, but we made the best of it. 'Poor Tom is gone,' he began, before pausing, trying to overtake what he thought I might be thinking. 'I'm not here as a politician. I'm here as Sean Doherty. He was a good friend to me when I was badly in need of friends. I'm sorry for your trouble.'

'I know that, Sean.' The reply was traditional, a convention. I did not know how to invest it with a meaning to convey to him that his sincerity was not in doubt. I grabbed his shoulder clumsily and gave him a vague embrace. My mother offered him a drink. He was off it; he would have a mineral. He sat drinking it in silence. Then he gestured towards me. 'This man here knows the story with politicians and funerals. But I'm here because I'm here. He was a great supporter of mine.' His sentiment, I knew, was heartfelt, but the language could not express it.

It soon transpired that Doherty's communication problem was not a figment of my imagination. He had been a TD in the constituency for twelve years, a poll-topper who had appeared to have acquired the state of political immortality. His support was not just loyal: it was fanatical. It had been forged in the hatred Doherty had evoked in the bosom of Dublin 4, and seemed well-nigh indestructible. But I noticed that a dramatic change had occurred since the last time I had taken serious soundings in the constituency. I had been aware that the sitting members – Doherty, Terry Leyden, and the Fine Gael TD, Liam Naughten – had run into trouble over the

Dublin political establishment's consensus about cutbacks in the health service. All three had uttered brave fighting talk on the issue, but in the end they had had to row in behind the 'national' consensus. The County Hospital in Roscommon was earmarked for downgrading in the near future, and plans for the closure of St Patrick's psychiatric hospital in Castlerea were well advanced. Already many of the staff had been transferred out of town, and patients were gradually being 'hived off' into what was known as 'community care'.

The town had been up in arms about all this for the past couple of years. Mass public demonstrations were held in the Square, and people travelled in large numbers to Galway to march outside the monthly meetings of the Western Health Board in Merlin Park. Doherty was unfortunate enough to be chairman of that body.

He had tried to take a stand on the issue, making vague threats about withdrawing his support from the government, but had been brought to heel by the party leadership. A couple of years before, at meetings in Tully's Hotel in Castlerea, he had declared that the hospital would be closed 'over my dead body', but now, with the closure imminent, Sean Doherty, though suddenly silent on the subject, seemed oddly alive. His line in private was that, since the closure now seemed inevitable, the town would just have to knuckle down and accept it.

But the town was doing nothing of the sort. The hospital had come to mean far more than its immense economic value to the locality. It was a symbol of the town's right to life. If it was closed, as someone remarked to me, 'they might as well build a wall around the town and let nothing in or out except the Guinness lorry'.

In the 1987 general election, the Roscommon Hospital Action Committee had put up a creditable showing with its candidate, Eithne Quinn; she received just over half the quota of first preference votes. This time, with a new candidate, a popular Roscommon publican, Tom Foxe, and the added edge provided by the amalgamation of the action committees from Roscommon and Castlerea, they expected, reasonably, to do substantially better.

I stayed in Castlerea for the next week, listening to what people were saying about the election. What I heard did not square with the analyses being put forward in Dublin. Whenever the Roscommon constituency was mentioned on national radio, on television or in the newspapers, it was merely to eliminate it from any calculations of what changes might occur. 'Roscommon? Two Fianna Fáil and one Fine Gael. No change there.' Occasionally a commentator would speculate that perhaps Fine Gael's sitting TD, Liam Naughten, might be displaced by his running mate, John Connor. But people locally did not seem to have heard that they were not supposed to be delivering any major shocks. There was an energy in the campaign that I had not felt there for years. Many of the people I had grown up with, who had previously supported one or other of the two main parties, were campaigning now for Tom Foxe. And the extraordinary thing was that they felt that he would be elected.

Ten days or so before polling day, I wrote an article for the *Sunday Independent*, saying that Tom Foxe would take a seat. A quietly spoken man, he had been a reluctant candidate. His demeanour was unassuming, though there was a slow certainty about him. He was in his early fifties, and had recently retired as an agricultural adviser. He had a good record in international boxing organisations. Foxe was not a politician, and did not know how to talk like one. But, when we met, he conveyed to me in his quiet way the strength of feeling he detected in the constituency. He felt certain of Eithne Quinn's 4,000 votes from last time out, and had a good chance of gathering another two or three thousand on the Castlerea hospital issue. He thought he would take Terry Leyden's seat.

My article never appeared: it did not coincide with the prevailing analysis in Dublin. In any event, as polling day approached, the picture began to change yet again. I noticed that people who previously would not have a bad word said about Doherty were now being openly disparaging of him. He had let them down on the hospital issue. He was 'only out for himself'. He was running for two jobs, one in Europe and one in the Dáil. 'Isn't one job enough for any man?' they asked. He had, they said, become arrogant, full of himself. He was rarely seen in the locality nowadays, and when he was there, he was brazenly dismissive of the people who had supported him.

One man, who had been on the torchlight procession nearly a decade earlier, met Doherty in the street a few days before polling day. Doherty greeted him by name. 'I suppose you'll be giving me the stroke.'

'I'm sorry, Sean. I'll be voting for Tom Foxe.'

'Well, you can fuck off so!' The defiance that Doherty had cultivated for his Dublin persona was spilling over into his home territory.

'And fuck you, too, Sean.' There was no irony in the reply.

Doherty had been concentrating on his campaign for the European Parliament, believing his home turf to be safe and in need of just a last-minute tweak. But as the day of electoral reckoning drew nearer, his mood of complacency was jolted, time and again, by the negative responses he was getting in his own heartland. By polling day he had become King Lear. Just after dawn, he drove up to the polling station in Castlerea, got out of his car and began tearing down and throwing in the nearby river Francis the posters displaying the plump and smiling visage of his running mate, Terry Leyden. A big hoarding with Mr Leyden's name in huge capitals was loaded onto the back of a tractor and driven away.

Throughout polling day, supporters of Doherty and Leyden were involved in sporadic outbreaks of bickering as the two candidates struggled to avoid being wiped out. The Foxe campaign was quietly confident. At one point, a Leyden supporter intimated to an overzealous Doherty campaigner that if he persisted in tearing down their man's posters, he would 'end up in hospital'. A passing Tom Foxe supporter, himself a former Fianna Fáiler, enquired, 'What hospital?' The entire place fell about laughing.

I had made up my mind to give my number one to Tom Foxe, and my number two to Doherty. My father, had he been alive, would have voted the same way. His sympathies would have remained with Doherty, but he would have felt very strongly the need to make a statement that would be heard loudly in Dublin, and understood in the precise manner in which it had been intended. When I arrived to vote, I found that my name had been crossed off the register. I had always voted here, I pointed out. It didn't matter, I was told; since I did not live in the town, I was not entitled to vote there: I should have transferred my vote to Dublin. I scanned the list, hoping to discover that there was some mistake. But my name had indeed been removed. My father's remained, as did that of my Uncle Martin, who had lived with us for some years. He had been dead since 1985.

On the day of the count I drove from Dublin straight to Roscommon. I had a job to persuade the editor of the *Sunday Independent* that it would be worth my while going; he wanted me to travel to Limerick. But then word began to trickle through on the radio about a 'surprise' in Roscommon. I got the green light and was off. On the radio, the voices were trying to make sense of what was happening. It looked as if Sean Doherty might be in trouble. There was talk of a 'protest vote' on the hospital issue having created the possibility of an 'upset'.

Roscommon, I reflected, just could not win. Even when we confounded the pundits, they had a way of making it sound like an aberration, a minor deviation from normality. They had imposed their paradigm on the country, had run the vast and complex aspirations of a people through the filter of their crude political perceptions, and had come up with an answer. If they made a mistake, it could not be a fundamental one, but merely a question of some quirk or vagary, some mad redneck behaviour that no educated person could have been expected to foresee.

When I walked into the count centre in Roscommon town, I immediately knew from Sean Doherty's face that it was all over. He was silent and impassive, but in the absence of reaction there was room for only one conclusion. He was wearing a black suit. He caught my eye and came over.

'A week ago you had your own trouble, now I have mine.' He reflected for a moment on this statement. 'Your trouble then was a lot worse than mine is now.'

In defeat, Doherty was still the star of the show. Everyone wanted to scrutinise his features for evidence of emotion, to absorb the drama of his defeat. Among the Foxe supporters, there was genuine bemusement at the very idea of their man having unseated the legendary Sean Doherty. They had targeted Terry Leyden's seat; the Doc was thought to be invincible. But Doherty's running mate had retained his seat; John Connor had retaken the Fine Gael seat; and Tom Foxe had been elected to the Dáil on his first attempt.

A party of supporters was sent down to Foxe's pub to collect their candidate for his victory speech; he was still pulling pints behind the bar. He came up to the count, heard himself declared a TD and made a short speech of gratitude to his supporters.

But Doherty appeared to have gone missing. The local Fianna Fáil director of elections apologetically took the microphone to announce that Mr Doherty had been 'called away on an interview'. He would make the speech on his behalf. A knowing smirk flashed over the crowd of several hundred people crammed into the Douglas Hyde Hall: 'He can't take his batin'.'

At that instant, Sean Doherty strode from the shadows. His face was slightly flushed, but he betrayed no emotion as he approached the microphone. The crowd fell silent. What would he say? What *could* he say?

In my pocket I had a copy of the *Roscommon Herald* for the week following the 1987 election. It contained details of the results and the speeches. My father always held onto crucial newspaper reports for future reference. I had been reading back over Doherty's '87 victory speech – a classic of Doherty-speak. He had scolded the two Fine

Gael candidates for the infighting which had marred their campaign. 'There were acts,' he had said, 'of grave political cannibalism. One situation was devouring another.' It was unlikely that he would return to this theme.

'Minister Leyden,' he began. His voice was steady and measured. 'Deputy Connor.' There were a couple of desultory whoops from the middle of the crowd. Sean Doherty paused. We craned our necks to catch this decisive moment of history. Doherty met the gaze of the crowd impassively. He was milking the situation for all its drama. There was no doubting that this was a politician in what is perhaps the truest sense of all: to him, losing was as much a part of politics as winning. Even in defeat, Doherty was the biggest draw of the day.

'Deputy Foxe.'

This was too much for the forebearance of the onlookers who immediately launched into an outbreak of whooping that was all the louder for having been held in suspended animation.

When the cheering had died down, Doherty addressed a few words to his loyal supporters. He spoke, in the exaggeratedly formal manner that had become his trademark, of the 'quite considerable ups and downs' he had experienced in his political career: 'Politics is not something I have expected any particular gain from.' They nodded. 'There are a lot of people,' he said, 'who are greatly saddened on this unique occasion in the political affairs of Roscommon.' They shook their heads in sympathetic disbelief. However, he wished to extend to the new-elected deputy, 'a deep word of congratulation'. He, Sean Doherty, had done his best to get elected, 'but there was another view expressed'.

Perhaps the expectation that he would be elected to the European Parliament on the following Sunday was contributing to the philosophical manner in which Doherty was receiving the news of his defeat: 'At the last election, I was the first deputy to be elected to the Dáil; maybe it was appropriate that I should complete a 360 degree circle and be the first man eliminated on this occasion. If I had got the same vote in the Dáil as I appear to have in the European election, Fianna Fáil would have got three seats.' (On the following Sunday, it transpired that he had failed also in his attempt to win a seat in Europe.)

Doherty concluded his speech on a black though hopeful note. 'We have,' he said, 'been down the darkest tunnel.'

Already in Doherty's mien could be observed the beginnings of a change that would take hold of him over the coming period. This change would manifest itself only when he was speaking to a crowd; when communicating with individuals, he retained his old ability to create sparks of recognition and familiarity – touching, slapping, winking, tickling, punching. But when faced with a crowd, he appeared to lose all his power, to withdraw into himself, to speak as though to strangers. He continued to talk in the same circumlocutory manner, his speech peppered with malapropisms and jargon. But, when he spoke in public now, there was little or no association between his words and his facial expressions, as though he did not know how to connect with a gathering of more than a handful. He literally had lost the common touch. In the coming months and years, as Cathaoirleach of the Seanad, Doherty, the politician, would continue to display a unique capacity for attracting unfavourable mention and publicity. There would be other 'scandals', occasional eruptions of GUBU, and no shortage of Dublin 4 outrage, no matter what he did. But he would no longer possess the ability to translate these into political capital on his own turf. Like a defrocked priest, he could continue to intone the words, to invoke the mysterious power, but he could no longer inspire the faith that would allow him to achieve the transcendence of the everyday which once had been at his command.

Throughout that long day of the count in Roscommon, even in the midst of our history-making, there were only occasional outbursts of triumphalism. The general mood was one of bemused reverence at the enormity of what had been achieved. On my way out during a break in proceedings, I met a Fine Gael supporter of long standing who was clearly pleased with the way things were going. Recognising what he presumed to be a fellow Blueshirt, he declared, 'Thanks be to fuck that Roscommon at last has digested Sean Doherty and shat him out.' I grunted and continued on my way to Foxe's pub, where the owner, and shortly to be elected Dáil deputy, was busily pulling pints. As I arrived, Sean Doherty came on the television set in the corner of the bar.

'Turn him up,' said a tightish voice at the counter, ''til we bury him once and for all.'

Doherty, live from the count centre half a mile up the road, adjusted his earpiece to hear Brian Farrell address him from the RTE election studio in the geographical as well as the spiritual heart of Dublin 4.

'Sean Doherty,' demanded Farrell, 'what went wrong?'

Doherty smiled his mocking, blue-eyed smile. 'Not enough people voted for me, Brian.'

Afterword
2011

Strangely, almost everyone who has mentioned this book to me, having read it when it first came out, remembers the title as 'Dancing at the Crossroads', with most of the remainder retaining it as 'Driving at the Crossroads'. I can understand both misrememberings: one fixated on the spectre of a dead patriarch, the other waylaid by the ghost of a long-crushed Hiace. Only a few remember the 'Jiving' part, which just goes to show: you can waste time thinking up smart titles.

It is strange to be given credit for something when you're not sure what you've done. *Jiving at the Crossroads* was like that. On its publication twenty years ago, in the autumn of 1991, it became an instant bestseller and remained in the literary hit parade for many months. Readers and reviewers praised it as a seminal work on the underlying conditions of Irish politics and the zeitgeist of the time. It was in large part credited with winning the *Sunday Times* Publisher of the Year Award for Blackstaff Press.

I found it fascinating that almost everyone who spoke

of it employed a different description. Some spoke of it as a 'social history'. Others referred to it as a 'memoir', or an 'autobiography'. Some read it as an essay, or collection of essays. Others even thought of it as a work of fiction, which has meant that occasionally to this day, when I am engaged to speak in public, I arrive at the venue to find myself described on the publicity handouts as a 'novelist'.

In this sense, that of category, I still don't know what to call it. It is not a novel, nor an autobiography, nor a social history. I might agree with 'essay', or even 'book of essays', except that essays tend to have explicit arguments and this book, while containing all kinds of micro-arguments, has no macro-thesis that I can give a name to.

Perhaps it is, then, in part a social history, in part a selective memoir, in part a novelised account of a life lived in 1970s and 1980s Ireland, through the medium of a relationship between a father and son that really spanned the cultural and imaginative trajectory of Ireland from the end of the nineteenth century to the beginning of the twenty-first. In constructing the narrative, I sought to speak for a younger generation that had been cast adrift on an ocean of new possibilities, retaining only tenuous links with the credos and values of its elders. It sought to make sense of all that was occurring in a frenzied time, to embrace what was new while retaining some respect for what was passing, if only out of love for and deference towards those whose version of reality was now being swamped by the incoming tide. Really, *Jiving at the Crossroads* looked back and asked: do we have to leave everything behind?

The period from approximately when I became a teenager in the late 1960s was one of momentous change for the public face of Irish society. I do not propose to rehearse these changes here, for we are surely sick of hearing about them. My main area of concern was that, ideologically speaking, the 1970s and 1980s were decades when it came to be believed that virtually everything that had hitherto been understood was based on error and ignorance. At this level – that of what might broadly be termed philosophy – *Jiving at the Crossroads* sought to lay bare the secret history of why things were happening as they were, and sought to place these events in the human context of a tangled and inarticulate love between a father who might have been from the nineteenth century and a son who might already have been in the twenty-first.

The 1970s in Ireland were a time of growing exhilaration, when it seemed to become obvious that the only things between us and freedom were self-imposed strictures and inhibitions. It helped greatly that cracks were beginning to appear in some of the institutions identified with holding together a traditionalist view of Ireland as a culture defined by certain ideas of nationhood, religion and outlook. The 1980s were characterised by a series of moral civil wars, in which issues like abortion and divorce became the defining questions of the struggle by then raging like a gorse fire on a Leitrim bog. At the time of the publication of *Jiving at the Crossroads*, the stage appeared to be set for a major re-evaluation of Ireland's direction and sense of self.

The book came about like this. I was reporting on the campaign for the 1990 presidential election, which was to result in the election of Mary Robinson. I was in an odd position: I desired victory for Robinson, but having been detailed to follow the campaign of the Fianna Fáil candidate Brian Lenihan, felt myself increasingly torn by a personal sympathy and liking for this loveable and – I felt, following his recent serious illness – vulnerable man. Although in my almost-daily contributions to the *Irish Times* I did not write explicitly about this personal dilemma, it became the subtext of my attempts to describe and analyse the campaign, and I suppose something of this crept into my reports and opinion columns.

After a week or two, I started getting phone calls from a writer colleague with whom I'd become friendly. This man, a poet of considerable distinction, had a profound passion for the nuances of Irish life and also an extraordinarily generous spirit in nurturing and encouraging voices he recognised as challenging or provoking him. Almost every day, he would call to speak about something I had written. Then, one day, after I had written an account of how Brian Lenihan's hand had become swollen from greeting people, the poet instructed me: 'You must write a book about this!'

A book about a handshake? It was a mad idea, and yet an intoxicating and endlessly fascinating one – provided I could keep the conversation going without actually having to put anything down on paper. I humoured him, while not taking the matter very seriously. But he persisted, saying that, with my permission, he would mention the idea to his publisher, Blackstaff Press. I thought that any sensible person to whom he mentioned the idea would give him a polite but non-committal response.

Soon after the election he came back to me and said that Blackstaff was interested in the idea. I had no idea what to do about this, or how to go about beginning a book, or even whether I had anything worth writing about. I had a sense that such a book would need to have an emotional core, but little more.

Reflecting more deeply on what the poet had perceived in my accounts of the election campaign, I began to have this glimmer out of the corner of my eye about my father and Sean Doherty and to make some kind of tenuous connection with the swollen-hand episode. I remembered the time when I had voted for Doherty, and this episode began to suggest itself as carrying something of the same content. There was something here worth telling, I intuited, but I did not think I could stretch it beyond a few pages.

The book came quickly, however – although even when it was finished it did not seem to me to be a book. It seemed to emerge from some logic of its own, rather than anything I recognised as any intelligence of mine. Thinking it would never see the light of day, I had taken a little too literally the advice of another helpful and encouraging poet friend of mine to 'write as if you were dead'.

For some time afterwards, when people asked me how long the book had taken to write, I would reply, 'Ten days.' But the sceptical response this provoked caused me to start disbelieving it myself. And yet, it seems to me now that the core of it was written very quickly. I would write one chapter at a time, often unsure of what was to follow until I reached the final sentence. Sometimes I put things in while remaining unsure why I was including them. Mostly they stayed in, even if I remained uncertain why they were there.

The elements of the book, beyond the personal story, were, it seemed to me, flimsily compiled around a vague sense of relevance to a certain time and a certain way of thinking. They loosely served the central story, which was about the relationship between a father and son, in which the drama of politics served as the sole common language.

The title came at the end. It refers, of course, to de Valera and the myth of his 'Dream Speech' of St Patrick's Day 1943, which popular memory refuses to believe did not include any reference to 'dancing at the crossroads'. For a long time, it was my second-favourite title. I wrote it and one other possible title on postcards which I placed on my mantelpiece and meditated upon for several weeks. I preferred the other one, but everyone I consulted voted for *Jiving at the Crossroads* and declined to transfer. The other title was *Darkness on the Edge of Town*.

I sent it off to Blackstaff, anticipating that they would write me a kind letter telling me that I had some potential as a writer and to bear them in mind if I ever wrote a real book. Within a week or two, the word came back: they wanted to publish it as it stood. Then I had to start worrying about how much of the book I could live with people reading.

When people speak to me about this book, they rarely mention the personal thread. They talk about the politics, the way Sean Doherty is described, the litany of my father's idiosyncrasies, the sketch of the structure of the town, or the analysis of how politics were handed on like a family inheritance. But they always seem to skirt around the matter of my father and me, the way we related and how this acted as the unifying thread in what they had read. That personal story is explicit and yet does not draw attention to itself as the primary element. Or perhaps the point is that this personal story allows itself to be absorbed without requiring any tacit admission on the part of the reader, who, because of the more public drama which the book shadows, is extended permission to believe that the core of the book lies elsewhere.

If you ask me what I think it is about, I may say something about the personal becoming political and the political emerging from the nucleus of personal relationship and feeding back in again. But really this book is a love story, which is why, I believe, people love it far more than I ever dreamed possible.

Jiving at the Crossroads, like most books, took on a life of its own in the mind of each individual who read it. For me it was less about Doherty than about politics as a language I had come to use to continue to communicate with my father, who, like many men of his generation, was consumed by the history and the drama of public events. Such events resonated loudly in the collective conscious-ness of Ireland then – in a way that already seems odd to those who grew up in more recent times – but they also became the very stuff of personal relationships. After you had exhausted the subject of the weather, you talked about politics. My father wasn't interested in sport and we were not great men for getting in touch with each other's feelings. What we had was politics, its dramas and its passions, and we made the most of them.

This, for me, was the point of the exercise, the emotional destination of whatever story the book might contain. Along the way, I sought to describe the reality of the country I had shared with my father for thirty-four years, the country he had introduced me to, described for me, remembered to me. In writing about it, I sought, as a primary imperative, to handle this country and his sense of it with as much tenderness as I could muster, while at the same time trying to be truthful to the perceptions I myself had gleaned in my thirty-five years exploring the same landscape. I suppose I sought to integrate my father's view of things with my own, to see if there was a language in which both views could be expressed at the same time, perhaps even within the same sentences, in a single perspective that did not require a straight choice to be made.

I began writing around that moment when my father and I walked out of the polling station in Castlerea and realised that, for what was ultimately the same reason, we had cast our votes for the same candidate: Sean Doherty.

From the outset I made clear my early antagonism to the political phenomenon that was Sean Doherty, and the core of the book consists of the reasons why I return to embrace him. Call Doherty a motif for tradition, if you wish, but he is also a cypher for the dignity of my father's relationship with the public world. The sense of nostalgia arises from the textures of this language and from the implicit awareness that it is all but impossible to re-create such a language without tearing apart the dreams and dignity of the old.

The story of *Jiving at the Crossroads* is simple: I grow in my father's shadow; I reject him; I tear myself away. And then . . . I return. Why? Because I have been driven back to my father's side by the false prophets of modernity. It is not that I reject modernity, nor even its prophecy. What I reject is the arrogance and ignorance of those who have appointed themselves to define it and lead us towards it. I reject the way they trample on the sensitivities of those I love and have regard for, not merely out of sentiment, though that too, but because this process destroys the cords that connect us through time to the consciousness and memory banks which, were we a more prudent people, we would be zealous to preserve.

Albert Camus said that if asked to choose between the most beautiful system of justice in the world and his mother, he would choose his mother.

The 'deeper' themes of *Jiving at the Crossroads*, therefore, relate this idea to a broader one: that a society, if it is to move onwards coherently, must remain respectful of the voices of tradition, not because these voices are necessarily wise and correct, but because they are loved.

Those who have read the book as some kind of apologia on behalf of Doherty and Haughey must surely see an extraordinary irony in the fact that, unwittingly and somewhat convolutedly, *Jiving at the Crossroads* was the spark that lit the fuse that was to end in the exploding of Charles Haughey's political career. I expect that, were they willing to acknowledge any such ironies, they would see this one as an accidental, collateral consequence, which must have filled its author with dismay. For the same reasons that they are wrong about everything else, they would have been wrong about this: I celebrate this manifestation of divine irony as I celebrate all others.

In December 1991, a few weeks after the publication of my book, I was asked by Shannonside Radio to take part in a live debate with Sean Doherty in its Roscommon studio, about *Jiving at the Crossroads* and the various matters raised by it. The producers were unable to enlighten me as to what line Doherty might take in the encounter, but I accepted the invitation. I headed for Roscommon with some trepidation, however, having become somewhat unnerved by Doherty's silence about the book up until then. For all I knew, he might have taken great umbrage at something I'd written about him and be planning to exact full retribution in public.

As it happened, he was very gracious, if characteristically watchful, committing himself on air to saying merely that the book was 'very interesting', a typical, loaded Dohertyism. He then went on to excoriate Charles Haughey, though, as was his wont in those years, deftly side-stepping several key questions he was memorably to address within the next couple of months. In the bar of the Royal Hotel afterwards, he winked at me and declared, 'For a minute there I thought we might have had a scoop on our hands!'

It brought me back to a day in the summer of 1988 which we spent out on Lough Key, near Boyle, in Doherty's speedboat. He had been his usual ebullient self, speaking in riddles and parables, occasionally veering into heavy sarcasm when the subject of Haughey was raised by me. Time and again, I pressed the issue: what was his relationship with Haughey like now? Was he angry that he had been excluded? Time and again, he smiled and praised his leader to the skies. As I boarded the train, I shook hands with the Doc and he stood there smiling until the train began to move. He walked alongside for a moment as the train edged forward. 'Off the record,' he said, 'I'll get that fucker if it's the last thing I do.'

The way Doherty saw it, his main sin had been loyalty to his leader, and this had neither been acknowledged nor rewarded. For him, all his alleged sins were down to, at worst, misplaced loyalty to his mentor and leader, Charles Haughey. There was some truth in this. The central, most coherent meaning for the colourful and mysterious events of what is known as the GUBU period resides in the political culture war which began with the Arms Trial and continued virtually until Haughey's death in 2006. It was all about Haughey, about the determination of those who had decided that he was the political anti-Christ to banish him from the political life of Ireland, and the resolve of his defenders to ensure they did not succeed. Doherty had from way back been one of his most loyal henchmen, centrally involved in the campaign to elect him leader of Fianna Fáil, which at the time ensured that he succeeded Jack Lynch as Taoiseach.

The notorious telephone-tapping incident, widely depicted as among the greatest stains on Haughey's 1982 administration, was either an outrageous abuse of office for party political purposes or an entirely justifiable attempt to protect the Taoiseach of the day from the subversive energies of his internal enemies. Doherty, like other ministers at the time, was concerned about leaks from the cabinet table, suspecting his longtime party rival, George Colley. In tapping the phones of two journalists, Bruce Arnold and Geraldine Kennedy, however, he stepped outside the party political arena and embroiled senior Garda officers in what undoubtedly was an illegal, as well as wholly bizarre, burst of activity.

That afternoon in the bar of the Royal Hotel in December 1991, Doherty fixed me with his ironic gaze and asked: 'What kind of a response have you been getting to my role in your book?' He said 'role' as though he had indeed played some part written for him by me. When Doherty spoke, it was both with a strange precision and a seemingly intuitive awareness that words merely allowed him to skirt along the tops of his desired meanings, which depended on the context and the cultural nous of the listener for the quality of their penetration.

I said that I had been getting four distinct responses: one was from people who said that I'd rehabilitated Sean Doherty and should be ashamed of myself; two, the people who said that I'd rehabilitated Sean Doherty and fair play to me; three, those who said I'd finally buried Sean Doherty and what had he ever done to me?; and four, those, mainly instantly recognisable Blueshirts, who said that I'd finally buried that fucker Doherty and a good thing too.

He pondered this for a moment before speaking. 'And, tell me, John, which of these objectives exactly *were* you trying to achieve?'

None of the above, I told him, truthfully. As far as my intentions concerning Doherty were concerned, I had set out with a simple objective: to explain why someone who was reviled as an untouchable in one part of the country could be hailed in another as a hero. I had wanted to explain the culture, more to myself than anyone else, from the roots up. And I had wanted to tell the story of the epiphany that had occurred in my relationship with my father, who had died two years previously, perhaps as a way of mourning him. The point of the Doherty elements had been to show how Sean Doherty became the means by which my father and I had come as close as we ever did to embracing each other. Doherty declared himself happy with this explanation and we moved on to other matters.

The next development I would regard as relevant to all this occurred just after Christmas that year. I returned to work at the *Irish Times* to find a large parcel in my pigeon-hole. It contained about a dozen copies of my book and a note from Terry Prone of Carr Communications asking me to sign them for a number of friends of hers to whom she wished warmly to recommend it. I signed the books and left them downstairs at Reception to be collected.

About three weeks later came *Nighthawks*. The programme, broadcast on a Wednesday night in January, was planned as a special on my book, which had been number one in the bestseller lists since its publication in October. *Nighthawks* was a then highly fashionable if somewhat 'alternative', even cultish, late-night TV programme, generally watched by an audience of a couple of hundred thousand young or youngish people, and featured the life of a fictional café bar run by Shay Healy, who played himself. Usually the fare was comedy, chit-chat and live music. It was broadcast on Tuesdays, Wednesdays and Thursdays. One of the show's features was a rolling, simple soap opera storyline, involving various regular characters and occasional visitors. It had been decided to build one such storyline around me and my book, the hook of which was that I had come up from Castlerea to meet Shay Healy, while he had gone down there to meet me. Castlerea featured because it was my hometown, and the place where the early part of the book was mostly set. The interview with Doherty was one of the Castlerea inserts. It was conducted in Hell's Kitchen, the public house and museum owned by Sean Browne, who had been a friend of both my father and myself.

Nighthawks was usually a live programme, which afterwards may have given an erroneous impression of spontaneity in relation to Doherty's intentions. In fact, the Doherty interview was one of several inserts pre-recorded in Castlerea over the previous weekend and slotted into the live show. I was in studio in Dublin on the Wednesday and, playing along with the soap opera gimmick, pretended to call Shay Healy in Castlerea from a deserted Nighthawks Bar. By my recollection, a brief interview with me was spliced into the pre-recorded interview with Doherty. This, as far as I recall, was the only element of the programme that actually went out live that night.

Why all this is relevant is that it is not possible to perceive Doherty's motivation for his subsequent actions without an understanding of the context created by *Jiving at the Crossroads*. I don't say this with any sense of self-importance, because, as it happened, I completely missed what he was up to, and indeed, when all hell broke loose the week after the *Nighthawks* programme, I wrote a column in the *Irish Times* saying that the whole thing was a bottle of smoke. He had been asked a series of fairly predictable questions, to which he gave the kind of answers I'd been listening to him give for several years. I had notebooks full of the kind of stuff he said to Shay Healy, and it never occurred to me that it might be worth committing to print.

Although I thought myself a shrewd Doherty-watcher, I really didn't cop that his game plan had altered from the wait-in-the-long-grass approach he had pursued for several years. At most I thought he was engaging in a little mischief, designed to raise his profile and boost his chances of regaining his Dáil seat at the next election.

In the *Nighthawks* interview, in fact, Doherty did not explicitly accuse Haughey of ordering or even being aware of the tapping of journalists' telephones in 1982. In a typical circumlocution, he said that he felt 'let down' over the fact that 'people' knew what he had been doing in the matter of the phone-tapping incidents. He elaborated somewhat as follows: 'One of the methods that was decided upon was the tapping of phones and anybody that says otherwise or tries to abandon himself or herself from that situation is not telling the truth.' This statement could be taken as referring to the other cabinet members, although a closer affinity with Dohertyspeak might have allowed it to be interpreted more specifically. As Minister for Justice, he was the person with the constitutional responsibility to deal with issues relating to questions of national security. In his capacity as Minister for Justice, Doherty explained, he had discussed the matter of leaks from the cabinet table with senior officers of An Garda Síochána. One of the proposals they put forward was the tapping of the telephones of specific journalists. He was asked to sanction this. He himself regarded the leaks as an act of subversion, at least as serious as those which had merited the tapping of the telephones of other journalists, under previous administrations in the past. (These had been concerned with journalistic contacts with individuals suspected of 'subversive' activity.)

Doherty's off-the-record position had always been that the government did not have any function in deciding on specific strategies in addressing the problem of the persistent leaks from the cabinet table. This was a matter for the Garda, at whose request, as the minister with responsibility, he had signed the order authorising the taps.

The most obvious inference from a literal interpretation of both the *Nighthawks* interview and subsequent statements by Doherty was that he personally decided on the phone taps in consultation with senior Garda officers, and received retrospective approval for this action from Charles Haughey. In the interview with Shay

Healy, he said he was 'required' to do this, an ambiguous construction which might mean anything along a line from a loose understanding of his duty to Haughey to a specific instruction from Haughey or someone else. For me it is suggestive of a relationship between Doherty and Haughey based on a form of mutually deniable mind-reading. Haughey's leadership style was very much hands-on, and indeed one of the criticisms levelled against both him and Doherty had been the allegation that Doherty's appointment as Minister for Justice was part of a pattern in which Haughey appointed people who would run their departments in precise accordance with his wishes and instructions, explicit or otherwise. Doherty's depiction of himself as 'required' to take action suggests a mindset in which he was aware of an unstated demand that something be done, a process that might, by the sound of it, have occurred in many other contexts as well. This, together with what he presented as Haughey's non-committal response when, as Doherty claimed, he was informed explicitly about the phone taps and handed the transcripts, amounted, according to Doherty's version, to an approval of his actions.

In one of the more convincing arguments put forward against Doherty's version of the phone-tapping issue, Catherine Butler, who was Haughey's personal assistant for ten years until his resignation as Taoiseach in 1992, suggested to Vincent Browne in *Village* magazine in 2006 that Doherty's version – that he had given transcripts to Haughey who had put them in his jacket pocket – was implausible because 'Mr Haughey never put anything in his pocket bar his silver comb, which he wore on the inside breast pocket and his handkerchief, which he put in his trouser pocket because he didn't want to ruin the line of the suit.'

Whatever the facts of the matter were about Haughey, it later emerged that Doherty had not intended to imply on *Nighthawks* that the cabinet, as such, was officially informed of the specific strategy of the telephone tappings, but rather that the matter was an open secret among cabinet ministers, and communicated to certain individual cabinet members on an informal basis. He was undoubtedly trying to give the impression that the Taoiseach, Charles Haughey, was one of those who knew what was happening, but in truth he had gone little further here than he had ventured before.

In the wake of the *Nighthawks* programme, there followed a week of frenzied media speculation about what Doherty might have intended to say, interpretations of what he did say, and analysis of why he said what he said when he said it, and did not say something else in some other way at some other time.

It was, I believe, the response to this initial interview that gave Doherty the idea that he might at last have an opportunity to settle his score with Charles Haughey. Safely back in Dublin having recorded the Castlerea inserts, Shay Healy and the *Nighthawks* team, with an eye to the potential for beneficial publicity, decided to cast their bread upon the waters and see if anyone would bite. Shay Healy made a few phone calls and established that, if interpreted a certain way, Sean Doherty's answers might be news. In advance of the programme, Shay's word-processor spewed forth press releases. The vacuum at the heart of the nation's post-Christmas newsdesks did the rest. By the morning of transmission day, the content of the Doherty interview was the subject of endless parsing and speculation. What Sean Doherty would say – what, in fact, he had already said – became the subject of convoluted analysis. In search of an angle, the media dug up a previous interview with Doherty, which, it was suggested, contradicted his latest pronouncement. Having initially sniffed the possibility of at last taking Haughey's scalp, the media became frustrated at the fact that, put under a microscope, Doherty's intervention had amounted to nothing particularly new. As the prospect of landing some big game began to diminish, the media began to turn on Doherty, inviting him to 'put up or shut up'.

For some time, Doherty said nothing, although the proverbial 'Sources Close to Sean Doherty' were being slightly more helpful. At one point in the week after the *Nighthawks* interview, Sources Close to John Waters had a conversation with Sources Close to Sean Doherty. Mr Doherty, it was indicated, was anxious that his words be taken at face value only. If he had wished to be more specific, he would have been more specific.

Because Doherty had been mouthing off for many years about how he was going to settle the score with Haughey, but had always seemed to shrink from the kill, I had no particular expectation that he would follow through this time either.

One afternoon the following week, my telephone rang. Sean Doherty identified himself. He sounded uncharacteristically sombre. He told me that if I came to the Montrose Hotel in Dublin later that evening, I might hear something of interest to me. I tried to engage him in conversation but he simply repeated the same message. Later, at a strange and nerve-racked press conference, Doherty said that Haughey had indeed known about the telephone taps and that he, Doherty, had personally handed him the transcripts of several such taps.

Haughey denied it, but the Progressive Democrats, Haughey's longtime adversaries and now his junior partners in government, demanded his head as the price for staying in the coalition. Within a few weeks, Haughey resigned as Fianna Fáil leader and, a fortnight later, as Taoiseach, to be succeeded in both positions by Albert Reynolds, whom he had not long before fired from his cabinet for leading a challenge to his leadership.

None of the political commentary that followed placed these events in their proper context, which was the changed and slightly more complex moral context created by *Jiving at the Crossroads*. Sean Doherty, I believe, read my book and got something from it that I had never consciously set out to offer him. Reading another version of the events with which he had been associated for a decade, he perceived that, even if his political rehabilitation was out of the question, it was possible to achieve rehabilitation of a more roundabout, cultural kind. *Jiving at the Crossroads*, by telling a story of his scapegoating in a culture divided over the personality of Charles Haughey, had given him a little of his confidence back, and the series of events initiated by its publication enabled him gradually to come to terms with the possibility of doing what he had long been threatening but might otherwise never have been provoked to carry out.

There are some senses in which Doherty was to blame for much of what happened to him. He was a scapegoat, but never quite a victim. He had a perverse streak in his character that caused him to play up to the role allotted to him by his enemies. He was so full of mischief and such a convincing actor that there were times when he seemed to be relishing the notion of himself as this crazed lynch-law-man, standing in personal judgement on his adversaries by virtue of his office. Part of the trouble was that the media presentation of Doherty as a crude tribal backwoodsman led his considerable intelligence to be underestimated, and this meant that nobody quite gave him credit for the complexity of his perspectives, or indeed for the mischief and irony that were his hallmarks for anyone who knew him reasonably well.

All of Sean Doherty's political 'sins' derive their weight from the sense they convey of someone in power operating on his own initiative rather than through the 'correct' channels. The tendency nowadays is to talk of such events as he became notorious for in purely legalistic, literal terms, but they are fundamentally about culture, which is all about perspective. The key moral questions related not so much to right and wrong as to which side you were on.

All this tension and drama was perhaps inevitable in a society which had lately moved from domination and dependency to taking its first baby steps in political and economic independence. The struggle that occurred in Sean Doherty's time was really between, on the one hand, those who through fate and circumstances had gleaned the resources to escape the implications of the past and, on the other, those who had been left behind to make their own way. The former demanded a new, shiny, exemplary modernity, while the latter perceived themselves to be still enwrapped in a history they could not so easily brush aside.

Perspective was everything. A lot of the indignation

about Doherty, and the demonisation arising from it, was simply a conflating of events into a particular set of meanings, which were, above all, convenient. This happens all the time in politics: events become important less because of moral content than political opportunity. I would not try to argue that the tapping of the phones of Bruce Arnold and Geraldine Kennedy was legally correct or otherwise justifiable. I merely observe that for some people, including Sean Doherty, such actions became less serious when seen in context. Perhaps Doherty's real mistake was tapping the phones of Arnold and Kennedy, when he should have been tapping George Colley's.

Some observers, calling in evidence of other events that subsequently cast dark clouds over the reputation of Charles Haughey, are inclined to bundle together all of these episodes – the arms controversy, the phone-tappings, the subsequent revelations about Haughey's personal finances – to demonstrate the validity of their wider argument. But what this approach overlooks is that the very existence of the culture wars created its own consequences. Nothing that happened can be assessed without consideration of the possibility that things might have happened otherwise but for the distorted conditions imposed by the efforts of a particular section of Irish society to wrest power for itself and set aside the democratic wishes of the majority. It has become impossible to argue with those who continue to excoriate Doherty and Haughey for both outlook and deed, but not entirely because the moral perspective of such detractors is irrefutable. A more critical factor is that they have won the war and so have succeeded in imposing their version of events and morality on the public realm and consciousness.

Sean Doherty's claim that he ordered the tapping of the telephones of Arnold and Kennedy on the basis that cabinet confidentiality was being breached, and that he wanted to discover who was breaching it, is easily dismissed in the culture created for and by the winners. It is literally impossible to argue because Doherty ended up on the losing side. To even try to explain Doherty's actions or personality in the language and logic of the re-created culture is inevitably to attract accusations of defending what is indefensible. But the justifications for his actions that Doherty offered appear more plausible and coherent when you see things from where he, and his followers and supporters, saw them. To that extent, the cloud that hung over him was in the eye of the beholder.

It was ironic, too, that, in the end, when Doherty and Haughey became adversaries, many of those who had been loudest in their fulminations against him suddenly turned and began defending Haughey against Doherty's lethal assault. This underlines two very interesting aspects of the culture wars: at one level it was as though whatever negativities Haughey and Doherty together represented were in some sense perceived to be more acute in Doherty than they had ever been in Haughey. But there is also the fascinating possibility that the anger of those who opposed Haughey was never really personal against him – what they mainly hated was that he had 'chosen' the 'common folk' over them. There is what you might almost call a psychosexual aspect: the Dublin 4 calumniators as jealous lovers, consumed with a neurotic rage against someone whom, really, they quite admired, or at least craved in some profound way, like a grandee craving a bit of rough. When the wedge became visible between

Doherty and Haughey, some of Haughey's most celebrated media detractors bizarrely rushed to defend him, at least to the extent of relishing the opportunity of kicking more determinedly his former friend.

This odd sociological drift was already discernible from 1989, in Haughey's late flirtation with the Progressive Democrats, in the wake of the election in which Doherty lost his seat. The utter extraordinariness of Haughey's alliance with the PDs is now almost forgotten. By then, he had become quite respectable, by virtue of being useful in relation to the handling of the economy. By the time Doherty came to wield the dagger, some of those who had longed for something like this eventuality for a generation suddenly found themselves torn between their current accommodation to Haughey for pragmatic reasons and their historical repugnance of him. Now, they were forced to choose between their immediate interests and what had once been their hearts' desire – the final removal of Haughey – a choice further complicated by the reminder effected by Doherty's intervention: that the Doc was the incarnation of most of the reasons they despised Haughey in the first place.

Haughey even briefly tried to exploit this tendency by playing to the fact that the prejudices of his own enemies were even more strongly pitted against Doherty than against himself. There was a remarkable moment in a press conference held by Haughey in January 1992 to respond to Doherty's allegation that he, Doherty, had told Haughey about the tapping of the two journalists' phones and had given him transcripts of the taps. Asked by a journalist if he thought Doherty's initiative was related to the leadership bid of Albert Reynolds 'and the so-called western alliance',

Haughey threw back his head, laughed and corrected him: 'You mean the *country* and western alliance!' For a moment, the hostility of the press conference dissipated and Haughey had most of the journalists again laughing and eating out of his hand.

As to whether Doherty's initiative against Haughey was, as rumour had it at the time, part of an orchestrated plot to open the way for Albert Reynolds, the evidence is inconclusive.

There is no doubt that Doherty's attitude to Haughey was by then such as to motivate him to act alone. It also appears that he chose a moment when he would be able to inflict maximum damage on Haughey, knowing that his statements about Haughey's knowledge of the telephone taps would put pressure on the Progressive Democrats to act on foot of their much-vaunted 'principled' approach to riding shotgun on the government, so making Haughey's position untenable.

Albert Reynolds has consistently said that Doherty was not acting on his behalf, that he did not put him up to it, and, in fact, that he did not regard Doherty's intervention as helpful to his leadership bid. But he said also, on various programmes in the week after Doherty's death in June 2005, that on the day the *Nighthawks* programme was aired he heard that Doherty was going to spill the beans on the show that evening and made strenuous efforts to contact him to dissuade him from doing so. Since the Doherty segment of the *Nighthawks* programme had been in the can for some days before the actual broadcast, and since Shay Healy and his producers had been assiduously leaking the contents to all and sundry over several days in advance of the broadcast, any account that Reynolds was given of what Doherty would say on the programme was likely to have been fairly precise. For the same reasons, it would by then have been too late to do anything to stop the interview. It is possible that, hearing of this unscheduled intervention, Mr Reynolds was chagrined to discover that Doherty was taking it upon himself to wield the dagger, perhaps sensing that any association with Doherty was more likely to damage him than otherwise. This would seem to add credibility to the substance of Albert's denials and point back to the lone-gunman theory. My own hunch, not least because he was frequently scathing about Albert's political capabilities, is that Doherty was carrying out a solo mission.

But there were those who believed otherwise. Sometime after all these events, towards the mid-1990s, I got a phone call from the journalist Veronica Guerin, at the time writing for the *Sunday Business Post*, asking if I would meet her to discuss something. I knew her reasonably well from various encounters on the journalistic beat, so I didn't give the matter much thought until we met, in Bewley's of Westmoreland Street, Dublin. Her tone, as we sat down, was serious – something I have sometimes observed in journalists when they are about to ask potentially tricky questions, a shift from the default tone of the profession, which is bantering and cynical, to a slight air of formality, as though the reporter has suddenly turned into a police investigator. Veronica said that she had to put to me a certain theory about my book, *Jiving at the Crossroads*. She had been told, she said, that the book had been written as part of an operation designed to remove Charles Haughey from office. I asked her who had told her this, but she declined to say. I asked her how it might have worked, and she said that the theory was that the book had been written to rehabilitate Doherty and give him the context from which to mount a credible attack on Haughey, using *Nighthawks* as the launching pad. It was obvious to whom such a sequence of events would have seemed desirable, but equally clear that the analysis was a *post facto* one.

I told her that I was as anxious as the next journalist to gain my place in history, and I wished I could tell her this story was true. Alas, it was utter fantasy. Looking back, it was just about possible to imagine such a sequence as she had outlined, whereas beforehand it would have been impossible to plan the way things evolved.

Doherty had known nothing of any intention of mine to publish a book about him, not least because I never had any such intention myself until sometime after I had finished writing it. The *Nighthawks* programme was after-the-fact, and completely unforeseeable. And, as far as I had known in advance, it was never going to be anything other than a soft promo-piece, with Doherty chipping in with some platitudinous remarks about my literary promise and perhaps a couple of judicious corrections of my speculations for the record.

We may never discover exactly what occurred, but it is unlikely that future historical detectives will be able to avoid the conclusion, based on the circumstantial evidence, that some degree of orchestration was involved in Doherty's final, lethal intervention, possibly without the direct knowledge or approval of the chief beneficiary.

In the wake of Sean Doherty's unexpected death in the summer of 2005, numerous references were made to the notion of his having 'found religion' in the last years of his life. It's something his friends would mention in a certain tone of understanding and respect. I heard the Taoiseach, Bertie Ahern, mention it at that time in what seemed to be a non-sequitur sort of way. But usually it was mentioned by his enemies, and usually also with the purpose of slyly attacking him in death.

For those who loathed Sean Doherty, the idea of his having 'found religion' had, not coincidentally, a peculiar and varied set of significances and meanings. One such explanation was that he had in some way 'repented' for what they would ironically describe as his 'sins'. Another was that his finding religion was an inevitable aspect of his political identity, which they would have characterised as 'conservative', among other things. The desired effect of such observations was usually discernible as the sly and vaguely subtle pigeon-holing of Doherty as a kind of craw-thumping latter-day saint, seeking to shake off his wicked past with rosary beads and pious ejaculations.

Such an impression would be about as far from the truth as it is possible to get. I knew Sean Doherty on and off for about two decades, and in that time never once heard him seek to atone publicly for any 'sins' he may have committed in his political life. Neither, in the years since he was supposed to have 'found religion', had I noticed any significant change in him. I remember meeting him once after having heard that he'd become a regular visitor to the House of Prayer in Achill, County Mayo, and studying him for signs of transformation. Happily, there were none. He remained the same incorrigibly mischievous, indiscreet and life-embracing man I had known before. Certainly, it was possible to perceive in his personality and conversation a harmonic of faith, hope and charity, but these chords did not sound new to my ear: he had always, it seemed to me, been a fundamentally decent man with strong beliefs and a staunch spirit in adversity.

There are few people I have enjoyed meeting as much as I enjoyed meeting Sean Doherty. He was a fabulous mimic and storyteller, full of gossip and interesting theories about developments behind the scenes of public life. To receive a phone call from him was to be invigorated by laughter, like a child being tickled. To meet him even for a minute was to be lifted for the day, to walk away chuckling and to carry with you a tale or two from the inside track.

The caricature of Doherty that had been created in the public mind by an implacably hostile media, therefore, extended to every aspect of his personality, including, towards the end, his faith and alleged religiosity. The demonic image of Doherty was as much the product of the secular antagonism he provoked as it was of the political sagas in which he became embroiled. The culture wars in which he featured so prominently in the 1980s and 1990s were fundamentally about the kind of Ireland that might be created in the then violently turbulent crucible of change. A central element of what was up for grabs was the spiritual ownership of Ireland, with those on the opposite side to Doherty/Haughey pushing hard to create a secular society in which the Catholic ethos which had dominated Ireland for centuries would be set aside. One of the reasons Haughey excited such opposition from the secular, liberal-left constituency was that he had nailed his colours to the mast by supporting the 1983 pro-life amendment, which sought to render impossible the introduction of abortion to Ireland by means of a constitutional amendment. It is inconceivable that he would have attracted anything like the odium he did if he had been a pro-choice politician.

So also with Sean Doherty. There are politicians who have committed far more grievous sins than Sean Doherty, but whose sins, if they have ever been noted, are forgotten by consensus of those who decide which wrongs are politically useful and which are not. Invariably in such cases, it will be observed that these forgiven sinners have all the while been careful to espouse the 'correct' positions on the things that matter in the ideological and culture wars that continue even after their consequences have come home to roost.

It is as difficult to communicate usefully about the good in a man who has been demonised throughout a whole culture as it is to avoid shivering while walking naked through snow. Every word you utter is dictated by the conditions of the surrounding climate, which in turn is the creation of those who, desiring to prevent the leakage of meanings which affirm their prejudices and prove useful to their projects, contrive to make any defence inadmissible or impossible. The demonised individual becomes an indefensible entity, not because of the facts, which may be long forgotten, but because of the daubs of prejudice which have been added, coat by coat, until there is nothing visible but caricature.

I met a man at Sean Doherty's funeral in June 2005 who told me about introducing a couple of his left-liberal-inclined friends to Doherty some years before, when the three of them were passing through Doherty's village, Cootehall. At first, he said, the two men shrank back as though even eye-contact with this monster would in some way shrivel them up. Unabashed, however, the Doc persisted in being the Doc, and, within half an hour or so, had both men rolling around in paroxysms of laughter. It was just one further episode underlining the strange inversion that has occurred in Ireland, whereby the new Pharisees who police our political culture are now the ones apparently steeped in an anal-retentive piety, while the supposed craw-thumpers have all the fun.